# the Southwest's Contrary Land

CRAIG CHILDS

FOREVER CHANGING BETWEEN FOUR CORNERS AND THE SEA OF CORTES

Arizona Highways
BOOKS

Book Designer: MARY WINKELMAN VELGOS

Photography Editor: PETER ENSENBERGER

Book Editor: BOB ALBANO

Library of Congress Control Number 2001086532. ISBN 1-893860-19-1

Map on page 3 copyright © 2001 by Robert W. Tope
Sketches accompanying the text were drawn by author Craig Childs in his field journals.

Published by the Book Division of *Arizona Highways*® magazine, a monthly publication of the Arizona Department of Transportation.

First Printing, 2001.

Publisher: Win Holden / Managing Editor: Bob Albano / Associate Editor: PK Perkin McMahon / Associate Editor: Evelyn Howell
Art Director: Mary Winkelman Velgos / Photography Director: Peter Ensenberger / Production Director: Cindy Mackey

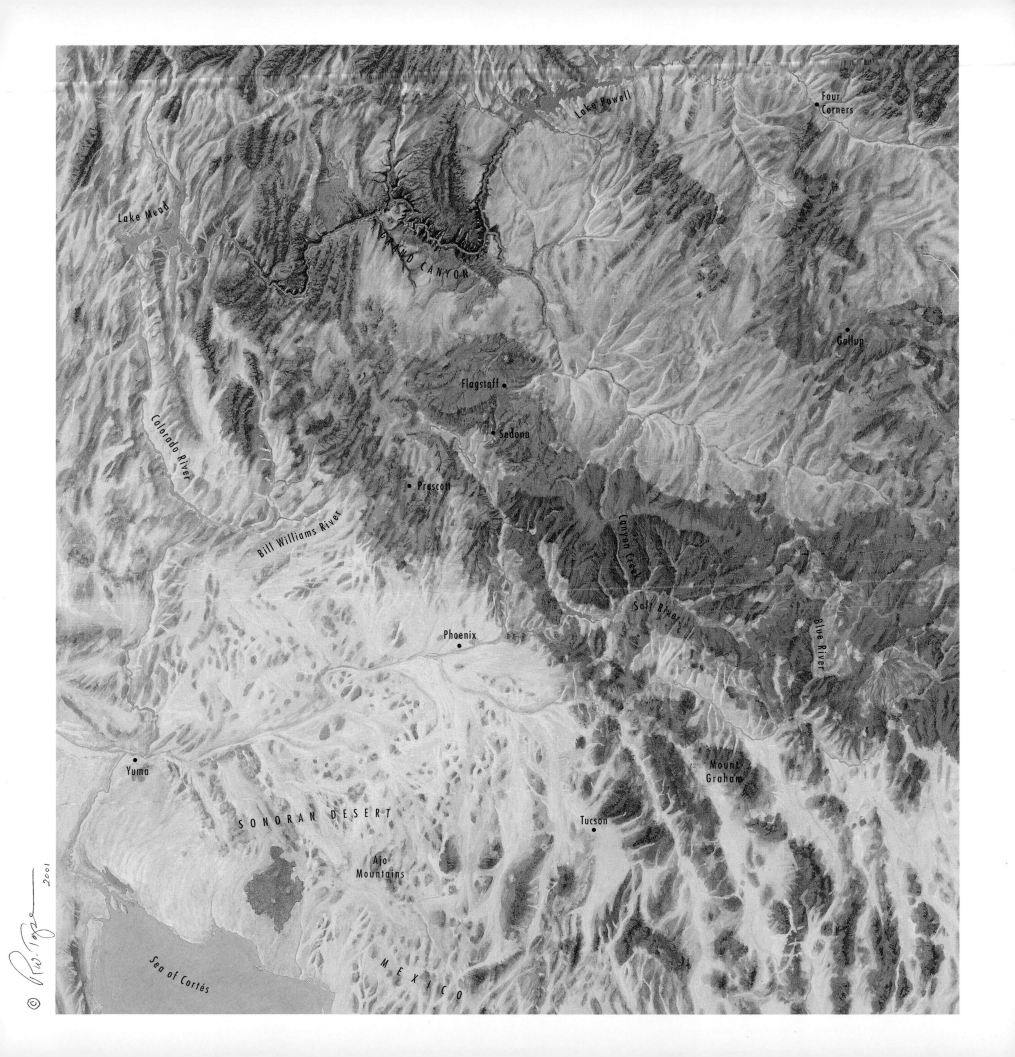

# CONTENTS

An aerial view of the lower Colorado River shows some of the looks that the Southwest takes on as it constantly reinvents itself. Here are low-lying desert peaks that roll into a strip of aquatic vegetation next to a river with water that came from mountains hundreds of miles away.

I always try for the window seat on airplanes. There are few other good reasons for flying. Over the Southwest, flying any direction from Albuquerque, Phoenix, or Las Vegas, I rarely stray from the small, oval window framing the world below. The landscape thrusts out ruggedness and contrast as waves of buttes, mountains, and canyons overtake one another, one flowing into the next. Viewing unending change and diversity at times has made me push against the window with both hands because I wanted out of the plane to be *in* the landscape, not *over* it.

On a recent flight across the Midwest, just past the eastern plains of Colorado, I spread tattered, spiral-bound pocket notebooks on the pull-down tray in front of me. An improvised jacket of duct tape kept one notebook from falling apart.

Here were the field notes for the book you now have in your hands. Here were records and observations from months of wilderness trekking. Here was the thirst that often accompanied the treks. And expectation. And cold nights on the desert floor.

One seat behind me was a girl, maybe eight years old. She had mistaken buttes in northeastern Colorado for the Rocky Mountains and her mother offered no correction. As we passed the exotic greens of Iowa, then Minnesota, the child said, "Now this is my kind of land, smooth."

She enunciated, *smooooooooth*, as if it had seven Os.

Hearing her, I smiled, thinking of how I could say the word "rough" with a guttural growl that would contrast with her sweet smoothness.

That is my kind of land. Rough. The Southwest. Rarely have I traveled beyond its borders.

When a traveler passes through the Southwest's environmental transitions, the customary description compares the trip to traveling from Mexico to Canada, referring to changes in climate and life zones. Taking more of the landscape into account, I would add to this description Kenya to Afghanistan, Dead Sea to Mongolia, and Patagonia to Brazil. And that would

not be enough. For certain Southwest landscapes seem to not belong to this planet. So diverse and wildly colored or shaped are they that I believe they cannot exist anywhere else in the universe. Only here. Only in this condensed span of geology and climate and humanity.

On my tray, sprinkled through mud-and-water soiled notebooks was my wish to tell the story of how the land lets go of one characteristic as it takes on another, and then repeats that pattern endlessly. Each notebook marked some great transition between environments or colors or textures of rock, where I had traveled from one place to the next, crossing thresholds. To fill these notebooks I walked many hundreds of miles, or in some cases only a mile or two.

I picked up one and read the first line I had written:

"The clicking of stones underfoot, boulders boiled into place from floods . . ."

I set it down and looked at the first line of another:

"Ravens do not at all have quiet wings . . ."

And a third notebook:

"A canyon caped in heavy March snow . . ."

Even months after I had written in these notebooks, the sensations I had experienced were still far stronger than my words. From 30,000 feet over Minnesota, I remembered the snow of a northern Arizona canyon, and wading through the water in the bottom, breaking ice with my shins. I pulled out my pen and a clean piece of paper and, writing on the tray table, began this book of transitions in a contrary land.

A ROUGH, WILDLY DIVERSE INTRODUCTION LANDSCAPE

Upstream from the Grand Canyon along the Arizona-Utah border, Lake Powell meanders among the sandstone tops of interlaced canyons of Glen Canyon. This locale is named Gunsight Bay.

# Following a Stream
# From Mountains to Desert

THIS IS HOW I REMEMBER IT.

JEFF SNYDER

I am 7 years old, holding a fishing rod loosely in two hands, creek water flowing over brown stones beside me. My father, in his 20s, is tying a leader line onto the rod's casting line. He uses a straight finger around which to make a nail knot. Some call it a blood knot, he says. I feel each of his tugs through the rod. When he finishes, he expects me to tie my own fly onto the end, a task that takes my small fingers about five minutes. Then he reaches into the creek, lifts a stone, and checks its underside for aquatic larvae. He gestures out with the cobble, pointing downstream.

"It's called Canyon Creek because there's a deep canyon down there."

I look downstream, between pines and cottonwoods. I glance back at my father, seeing that he's got this far-away look, somehow seeing the bowels of this creek 20 miles, 70 miles away.

"All the way to the desert," he says. "Big cliffs and a narrow, dark bottom. Wild land down there."

He picks out a fly for himself. An elk hair caddis. "We'll go down some day, get inside that canyon."

I look down the creek, and my imagination bursts open like a magician's box. Shadows shifting against each other in the winding depths of cliff and creek. Madhouses of boulders and waterfalls. Somewhere down there.

□  □  □

Now 32 years old, I walk with two friends, each of us wearing packs laden with two weeks of food and gear. Meadows roam alongside cold creek water, fringed by thick stands of ponderosa pine, white pine, and Douglas fir. In the forests, massive elk antlers lie discarded and cluttered with branches and rotted trees. We drop our packs, and I walk to the water where it runs clear and swift across a shield of bedrock. This is the place. Canyon Creek at its headwaters.

I stop and bow my head. The lullaby of the creek has always relaxed my muscles, made me close my eyes to listen more intently. The sound is not the roar of urgent water, and it's not the plucking of a tiny stream. It is the ornamental singing of an Arizona creek beginning its way from the mountains to the desert.

In my right hand I carry a sack heavy as a bag of granite. My father's ashes.

One friend, Keith Knadler, a river guide turned stock-market trader, reads aloud from his journal, something about death and cycles. I listen, then reach out with the bag and pour the remains of my father into Canyon Creek.

He had never made his way to the remote, inner canyons below here. When I sorted through his belongings at home after his heart attack, I found heaps of maps rolled, folded, and stacked as if obsession had driven him to do so. Sometimes the same map had been purchased four or five times, folded and refolded until the paper turned soft as wool. He had pored over the topography, figuring out ways of getting inside the canyon. But he did not go.

So I come now with his maps and the memory of his words about why Canyon Creek is so named.

His ashes briefly cloud the downstream water. The current sorts the bone fragments, feathering them into safe places — behind a rock, on the outside edges of a quick current, across the fluted sand in a pool. The creek uses his bones to spell out its intentions and directions. My father, now a subject of fluid mechanics, becomes more than ever a student of the creek that he fished since before I was born.

"Done," I say, shaking out the last of the ashes.

My other friend, Irvin Fernandez, an assistant manager of a national wildlife refuge, says, "Just beginning."

We travel from that point, humping gear onto our backs, aiming into the canyon my father had imagined. We begin walking along Canyon Creek from its start at a cleft of the Mogollon Rim to its confluence with the Salt River more than 100 miles below in the Sonoran Desert.

☐   ☐   ☐

The weather on this February day was warm at 7,000 feet. Banks of snow dirtied with pine and spruce needles had been whittled down, surviving only in the most shaded places. Four feet of snow may fall in a single storm up here, but the place differs from the mountains of more northern states such as Colorado or Montana. Often the snow here melts substantially during the winter, frequently leaving even the highest elevations bare. Only 10 percent of winter's snowfall actually feeds the creeks of the Mogollon Rim. The rest fades into the ground. It has always been a wonder to me that the creeks here — Cherry, Canyon, Cibeque, and the like — flow as strongly as they do in such a dry, alpine region.

Mostly, this creek draws its water from springs. A share of the winter's snow is deposited in underground banks that eventually spill out of the slopes beneath the Mogollon Rim. Some of the springs flow north, feeding the Little Colorado River, eventually reaching the Grand Canyon. But most head south to the Salt River 4,500 feet below.

Along the 200-mile length of the Mogollon Rim's south side, 80,000 gallons of water emerge from the ground every minute. The largest spring on the rim, far to the west of Canyon Creek, puts out 18,500 gallons per minute. The water tends to be clear, much lower in salts and dissolved minerals than the desert springs that give the Salt River its name. The purity of the water matches the purity of my memories. My father and I fished this creek together for 25 years.

On the third day down Canyon Creek we crossed fallen bridges of Douglas fir as we sank through steep walls. Dense

JEFF SNYDER

The opening spread (Page 10) shows Canyon Creek making its way from the Mogollon Rim and cutting through the desert. It also shows the stream's smooth cobbles and a distinctive cliff formed by the erosion of sediments.

Maple trees, opposite page, favor the Mogollon Rim with a splash of fall color.

Distinguished by pure water, Canyon Creek, left, adds a riparian touch to a sloping meadow below the Mogollon Rim.

13

From this vantage point on the Mogollon Rim's southern edge, one can see the lavish blanket of green nourished by snow and rain water flowing from the rim.

timber rose up the canyon sides, occasionally revealing streaks of cliffs. This site was below the places where my father and I had fished. New country. Bigger boulders and sharper drops presented themselves as meadows surrendered and swirled into short waterfalls.

Smells billowed into the air — the must of animals and the heavy scent of garden loam. Wrinkled, dried canyon grapes released a sweet, fermented odor. A storm arrived in the late afternoon while I fished for dinner. Thunder. A throaty boom followed by echoes testing themselves through the canyon, rounding into smaller side canyons, rattling into the trees. Six months had passed since I last heard thunder, back when my father was still alive. This was a moment to appreciate.

The sound of thunder entered certain cells in my brain, those old and otherwise dormant. My skin prickled and my bones and stomach felt the vibrations. A sheet of hail immediately followed. The stream bubbled with impacts, and I held my rod still. No sense in fishing, or moving. Water braided off my hat brim.

I had stood like this so many times in the past, shrouded in thunder on Canyon Creek, motionless, my rod in my hands. Usually at these times my father had been a mile or so from me, alone on a creek boulder doing the same thing: listening to the graciously violent sounds of the storm, smelling the air, waiting.

When the rain slowed, I cast, sending out arcs of line. I cast below damming rock piles, into the good places where my father taught me trout feed. The thunder became guarded, grumbling away. Now drenched and darkened by clouds, the forest was opulent in shades of green.

When night came, bringing heavier rain, the three of us set a tarp and crowded beneath it with our sleeping bags, taking half an hour to get situated, trying not to become soaked. With hiking boots stowed, turned upside-down so they would not collect water, we sank into our bags. Lightning continued into the night, burning the air with crisp, blue flares of electricity. Strokes of thunder put me to sleep, and I did not awaken until dawn, when

15

RAIN IN THE FOREST

Between the two, the Central Highlands functions as a transition zone where you find formations from the Grand Canyon bending down to the lowlands, then buckling to pieces. This region is the breath that the land takes as the characteristics of one territory give way to those of another. Canyon Creek runs the entire length of that breath.

Up top, at the headwater meadows, plant species number around 200. The number falls over the next 100 miles — a 4,500-foot elevation drop — until the species are reduced to a little more than half that number. The calypso orchid, mottle-leafed rattlesnake-plantain, and spring-flowering coral-root growing among moist sedges are replaced with devil's claw and brittlebush, which grow from bare, sandy ground.

The slopes and canyon sides above the creek shed their forests and montane plants, while the creek bed is still immersed in forest. Cold air tends to drain down the canyon alongside the creek, keeping the low forests cool and moist. So the prophesies of the desert are first told up high, away from the creek, and on the warm, dry southern faces.

Without patience, a traveler would not notice the changes. Even a day or two of walking does not show startling contrast. Transitions advance and retreat like tides, but eventually they make their mark.

Recorded in my notes, the first appearance of manzanita came about the same time as sharp-tipped agaves and heavy, stunted oak groves. Then the first sycamore tree, bold by the creek. Ponderosa pines belong to the broad, sunny valleys, Douglas fir and Engelmann spruce to the canyons. Narrowleaf yucca, banana yucca, and the painfully barbed wait-a-minute bush, *Mimosa biuncifera*, appeared in the forests. Scrub oak and mountain mahogany took the dry, south-facing slopes, hinting at the desert below. But the desert was far away. Heavy timber still dominated the canyon.

I came to the creek alone one evening to gather water. Lurking among the shades and shapes of the very last light, I had the same eerie feeling as one gets from reading three chapters deep into a murder mystery. Moving water obscured sounds from

remnant clouds of the storm's calm tail haunted the forest.

□   □   □

The tones of running water deepened and hissed as the landscape tightened. Penned by canyon walls, the creek became more resolute and turbulent. This region belongs to the Central Highlands, bordered to the north by the Colorado Plateau, to the south by the Basin and Range Province, a low-lying desert pocked with unconnected mountain ranges.

Geologically, the northern region of the plateau extends all the way to the Grand Canyon, to Zion National Park in Utah, and to the red sandstone canyonlands of the Four Corners with an orderly lay of rock formations as uniform as stacked books.

The province to the south is a mess of tilted blocks and pieces of ground interspersed with the rocky remains of ancient volcanic plutons.

Waters of streams such as Canyon Creek represent only about 10 percent of the water generated in their birthplace on the Mogollon Rim; yet their flow remains strong, moving so quickly in places that it appears milky to a camera that cannot stop the water's motion.

17

Near its headwaters, Canyon Creek flows through an area that supports some 200 species of plants, such as the yellow cone flower.

the forest. Chambers among trees faded into further darkness. Animals could be moving, and I would not see them.

I dipped water bottles into the creek and looked up at the black forms of Douglas fir sprouting into the sky. Returning to camp, I heard the comforting mumble of voices, casual conversation in the making of dinner. This closed the murder mystery. I joined my friends.

The next morning came cold with beads of ice around the cavernous entrance to my sleeping bag. Sunrise was not warm enough. Irvin coaxed a fire out of damp pine needles and rain-wet twigs. A little bit of flame came of it. Mostly smoke. We stood and crouched around it, letting the smoke permeate our hair and clothes and fingernails.

This day of walking had brought our first sotol, a studded ribbon-leafed member of the agave family, and a gangly cactus called Whipple cholla, *Opuntia whipplei*. We purposely did not speak much of the desert and its cactus far from here. On a trip like this, distances are too far to be openly discussed, and boundaries are difficult to define. We knew the desert would arrive as slowly as the forest would leave, and in places they would overlap.

Days earlier we had passed onto the Fort Apache Indian Reservation. Permits were carried in my pack should we encounter an official from the tribal government or a rancher out seeking lost cattle, but we found no fence or sign to delineate the crossing. So we refrained from discussing artificial boundaries such as Apache, desert, or national forest. We only talked about what we had seen, sitting up into the night recounting stories to each other: bald eagles we had witnessed commuting up and down the canyon; a coyote's glance before loping away; trout in a pool; in a side canyon, an hourglass arch 100 feet tall, one of those elliptic, symmetrical, female arches, a landmark we were sure had never been recorded on a map.

That night we made camp in a narrow tumble of a canyon. The creek poured and leaked between half-cocked boulders three- and four-stories tall. When we talked about what we had seen that day, we discussed the geometry of black

Lying under stones, left, in Canyon Creek is aquatic life that tells fishermen what type of fly to use in their quest for trout. Alongside the creek, above, the rocks serve a more artistic purpose by displaying patterns and colors.

19

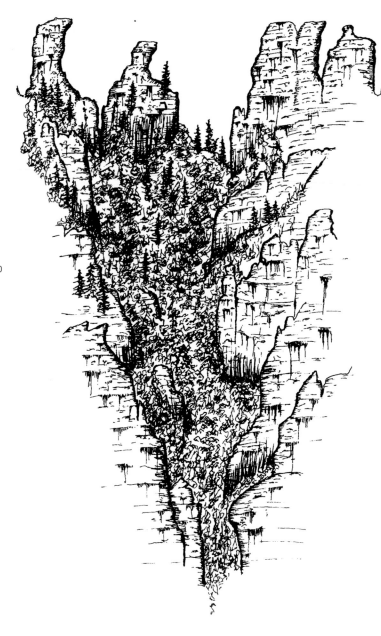

Vegetation in the
water, opposite page,
lends a greenish cast to
a pool below a small
riffle on Canyon Creek.

rock art in a side canyon. Most likely, the art was the work of Apache. Keith drew lines in the air, commenting on red artwork he had found on another rock wall nearby. Probably much older than the Apache work, the red artwork came from a culture known as Salado, or perhaps the Mogollon people, 700, 800 years ago.

"And my father coming downstream with us," I said as we sat in the sand between boulders, each taking a turn stirring soup for dinner. "He would have appreciated these places, hidden caches of rock art."

Nods from my friends indicated agreement. They had known him. Keith, Irvin, and I had returned from many treks together to tell him stories, to tell him about lost canyons and cliff dwellings. While he fixed meals for us in his kitchen he always listened attentively and asked important questions. They had seen in his eyes that he wanted to be out there with us, but it was too cold, too hot, too rough, too dangerous; and where we usually traveled in the desert there were no trout. So he never came with us because he was a fisherman. He only sat and listened to our stories of places wild.

As we talked about him, I was again stunned that he was dead, that such a striking transition had been made so suddenly from a breathing, moving man to a bag of ashes.

I figured that he had to die to come into these interior canyons with us. It was easier this way. He could float his way through. He was free, and I imagined his bones, spread over miles, tumbling through riffles, sinking to the bottom of pools, catching among broken alder branches and stacks of waterlogged sycamore leaves. I thought of him as playful and ecstatic with the water. The finest dust of his ashes flushed into the dizzy bubbles of waterfalls.

Transformation is a primary element. I see it constantly in landscapes. I spend my life walking through transitions, witnessing them in the spread of forests reaching deserts, and mesas leading to canyons to playas to basins. Now I see it in human life.

After dinner we went to our sleeping bags, stuffing ourselves into spaces left between water, boulder, and cliff. I slept on sand,

MOGOLLON RIM
TO THE
SALT RIVER

JEFF SNYDER

As Canyon Creek nears the Salt River, saguaro cacti crop up on the stream's rocky slopes.

the
Southwest's
Contrary
Land

22

atop the tracks of a mountain lion that had walked through that morning.

□ □ □

Light snow fell like lace from the sky, hardly enough to gather on the ground. We moved into the most cramped canyon thus far, making delicate maneuvers across boulders over swift, deep reaches of creek water. Briar patches of flood debris, fallen trees, and thorn-covered vines took us down into the roaring hollows. We spider-climbed the walls, and at one point I pulled my pack off and passed it to Keith, my right hand crammed into a hold, my left hoisting the pack over the water. Keith took it from below, but lost his hold in the transfer of weight. In a graceful arc, he made a pendulum of my pack, sending it around to a dry rock, while tossing himself fully committed into the creek.

An hour later Irvin took a bad step and landed on the angle of a boulder, which delivered him like an arrow into the water. And an hour after that, according to schedule, I leapt toward the dorsal fin of a mid-creek boulder. I hesitated as I sprung toward the rock, and I missed it.

The left side of my jaw took the first impact, hammering against the place where my feet were supposed to land. Then a swatch of skin came out of my right knee on another rock as I toppled halfway into the creek, the weight of my pack shoving my face into the water. As I wrestled back up I noticed that on the rock where my face hit I had left a smear of saliva. I swiped it up with a finger and showed it to Irvin.

It was not necessarily clumsiness that had us falling. It was just that the terrain had many complexities, testing our grace at every move. This is what my father had meant when he got wild-eyed and gestured down the creek when I was little. He never saw them, but he had envisioned these dinosaur walls and monumental boulders tumbled on edge. I never talked to anyone else to find out if such a canyon was here. I never read a guide book. I always knew that he was right. It would be here.

I sat for a moment to pad the blood off my leg, and I spoke out loud, "Here it is, Dad. Just like you said."

This is the place, I told him. Raked by floods, trees busted

and splintered, boulders lopped all over each other at the bottom, mud and debris packed into my boots, his bones drifting down day by day. This is what a canyon is supposed to be: a place where everything is drawn to a sharp point, every emotion and physical detail.

Toward the end of the day, after we saw our first mesquite trees and bushes of cliffrose, as pine forests on the high rims thinned into junipers and oaks and piñons, the canyon began to bend open slightly. Cliffs broke into rectangular towers and massive blocks of 90-degree angles. The place had the look of construction, like cities — New York skyscrapers built wall to wall with one narrow strip below where the water flows.

At the floor of the canyon we set an evening camp. The creek fell into bedrock, opening cylindrical tubes and slots in the floor. It was a camp loud with the brace of fast-moving water, where we spoke loudly to tell our stories, where we asked questions of each other: why do we crave this kind of physical, geographical madness?

"That spit Craig left on the rock where he fell," Irvin said. "Now that stuff was real."

Keith agreed by holding out his hands, showing us how scraped and cracked they were. "This whole place — moving through it — is very real. You can feel it right here, in your hands."

Again we found our places, and we slept to the roar.

□ □ □

Canyons undulate along the length of the creek, tight in some places, and in others open to juniper stands and grazed pastures. After a brief opening into mesquite bosques and gnarled stands of oak, the canyon crimped down again. The walls became studded with tiers of rock columns, and the water closed to burbling echoes and the loud hush of chutes into pools. This ninth day brought jojoba, the crucifixion-thorn, barberry, the big catclaw known as *Acacia Greggii*, and a host of other sharp, spiny unfriendlies indicative of the thorn-scrub environment of the Sonoran Desert.

Huge, angular chunks of geology were broken and half-

23

A thirsty landscape stretches out alongside Canyon Creek and begins to pen it, forcing its waters to speed up and become more turbulent.

25

Erosion makes these
soft, volcanic rocks on
a forested slope seem
to be coated with
minerals.

sunken in the water. This was the bass note of the entire length of Canyon Creek. It was the low drumming of water through boulders and tunnels.

A massive spring entered from the east wall, making way for lettuce heads of riparian vegetation — watercress and ridiculously fat leaves of columbine flowers and meadow rue. The color of the creek changed where the spring entered, becoming crystalline green. I had come to this spring years earlier, fishing its clear pools. At the time I was traveling cross-country alone for eight days on only peanuts and beef jerky, so it was important to catch a meal as I passed the creek. What I caught then was a trout of a species I had never seen, perhaps an Apache trout, or a Gila trout, or some hybridized combination of native and non-native. Whichever, it was likely an endangered, protected species. At the time I put it back and returned hungry to my trek.

The Apache trout, *Oncorhynchus apache*, of eastern Arizona's White Mountains, was placed on the endangered species list in 1967 and later "upgraded" to the threatened species list. It is now being produced in hatcheries. Before that, it was known that an unnamed native trout existed in the region, occasionally found in creeks ranging from above Sedona to New Mexico.

Another native, the Gila trout, *Oncorhynchus gilae*, had only been identified in 1950. It, too, has been heavily pushed back by introduced sport fish, livestock grazing impacts, development, over-fishing, and human water use.

Perhaps the only reason the Apache trout still exists is that the White Mountain Apache tribe in 1940 closed the Salt River headwaters to fishing and stocking. One biologist who studied this trout's chromosomes to distinguish it as its own species, named it Apache to honor this early conservation work.

Canyon Creek is not one of the protected streams on the reservation, although upstream it is limited to artificial fly fishing only (my father once stole a yellow "fly fishing only" sign, bent, rusted and barely legible, to hang in his tool shed). The headwaters of Canyon Creek flow through an Arizona Game and Fish Department hatchery, built to rear primarily Arctic grayling, rainbow, brown, and cutthroat trout, mostly non-native to this

creek, easily nudging out any native species, or hybridizing them toward extinction.

After a 1995 renovation, the hatchery aimed at producing 150,000 pounds of fish a year. Few of those pounds actually swim this far downstream. The high desert environment inhibits trout with water too warm. In fact, land below 6,000 feet is generally poor for trout, so this cold, oxygenated spring is an oasis. The exact species of trout here still evades me. These days, the Apache trout has not been seen as far west as Canyon Creek, restricted to the upper-elevation creeks around Baldy Peak. But then, not many fish biologists venture into this lower domain.

When I think of the rare and unknown fish, and each of these isolated creeks, I am reminded of the solitude of this country below the Mogollon Rim. This must be why my father originally came — just before I was born — and why he continued to come until his death. His love for fly fishing verged on magical. He believed so strongly in this territory and what it held that he could not escape it. To be honest, this is tough, nasty trout fishing here. The creeks are so small and variable in their flow, and so cluttered with boulders and fallen trees that it is like trying to fish inside of a cave. He called one of these creeks Cruel Creek. He spoke fondly about the richness and frequency of trout waters in Colorado, and he could have gone. But he didn't.

When I reached the spring, I pulled out my rod to catch a trout and get a closer look at it. I tried the waters around the

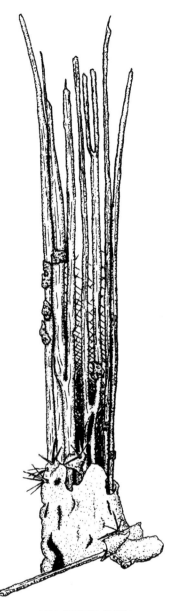

DEAD SAGUARO CACTUS

Canyon Creek, after twisting for more than a hundred miles through forest, canyon, and desert, flows into the Salt River.

29

NORTH FACE RIDGE
OF UNNAMED CANYON

stopped and watched it. Within the light were the darker motions of trout darting and rising.

It was four years earlier that I had a dream of my father leading me into the desert, then underground to a secret cache of running water. It swelled up from below, colored with an unaccountably rich, green light. In my dream the color was overwhelming. It was unmistakable. My father fished into it and presented me with beautiful, strange catches.

I had been in the backcountry when I had this dream and I wrote it in my notebook, tearing out the pages and giving them to my father the next time I saw him. He read them and told me he thought things like that were true, that there was illuminated water issuing from the earth. I told him about the quality of water from my dream, how I had never seen anything like it. He smiled. He was pleased with this dream and the color I described.

It was the same color below the spring. This light. This water. I stood and stared as trout moved in and out, their forms rippled and folded by the water. I could hardly believe that it was the same, a color and light I had never seen before in any other creek. I cried. A good, solid cry, eyes open. Astounded, confused, amazed. I knelt at the creek side and scooped water with my hands. I washed my tears into Canyon Creek. A message to my father.

☐   ☐   ☐

On the morning of the 12th day, I sat with my journal, writing under the first hints of daylight. With three fingers on my writing hand bandaged together as a splint, it looked as if at least two were broken, another slightly swollen and discolored. I had fallen 15 feet out of a crack onto my backpack like a turtle upside-down, my right hand caught between the pack and the ground.

We were all taking the journey hard. The elastic branches of alder and willow trees had delivered constant, concise smacks to the rim of the nostril, the knuckles, the lips, the outside edges of the ear. Blood was drawn by catclaw and rock and the battering rams of woody manzanita branches. I noted one day in my

spring, caught one trout, but lost it in a waterfall. Trying to maneuver between boulders, I fell and broke the tip from my rod two eyelets down. Difficult fishing. I put the gear away and walked to the spring. Hovering serene in the pools were at least 30 trout. There was a remote chance that these fish had never been seen, a species yet to be named, isolated for decades, centuries, or millennia in this low canyon spring.

Below here, two huge boulders had fallen against each other into the creek, leaving the water deep between the two. The angle was just so that sunlight rose from underneath, giving the water a deep, emerald glow. It was more radiant than colorful. I

Just before joining the Salt River, Canyon Creek finds a flattening landscape and room to stretch out and rest.

journal that a bayonet of agave rammed straight through skin and into the muscle of the calf produces a remarkable call to attention. As Keith said, we were being pierced. Cuts and rips and abrasions and lacerations. With two broken fingers, I wrote in my journal slowly and with big, sloppy letters.

The morning arrived with relative warmth. No ice. On cold mornings we remained in our bags longer, timid about showing our flesh to freezing air. Each day as the alpine environment slipped away behind us, we rose earlier to warmer mornings.

Within a few hours of camp, the canyon opened again, revealing the granite floor of the desert, giving us our first ocotillos, then a paloverde tree. In the next few miles the bulk of the canyon became salt and pepper granite carved by water into hooks and curves as elegant as whale flukes. Waterfalls stacked into each other over olive-green pools of unknown depth. Keith tested one, dropping his pack and standing naked

THE LOW COUNTRY

on a polished granite promontory 25 feet above the water. He dove and the white flash of his body sailed underneath into the dim, deep water. He emerged with a gasp. He had not found the bottom.

Passage through the granite turned out to be more difficult than we had planned. The rock was beautiful and sleek, but relentless. Sheer domes had been smoothed by running water. Handholds were difficult to find. On one exposure, Keith just danced his way across. It was a delicious maneuver to witness, his body wavering like a blown willow. It also scared me to my core to watch him do it. Irvin flattened his entire body to the rock and inched across on toes, knees, chest, and fingers, substantially less graceful. This scared me more.

I don't know exactly what I did when I got there, but it was done poorly, and payment for my crossing would be two ribs dislocated, visibly out of place like thrown rods. I was above the creek by 20 feet, barely adhering to this curve of rock, the weight of my pack drawing me down. Midway out I lost my faith. My hands crept around, looking for something to hold, and my face went flush against granite.

"I can't find anything," I gasped. Irvin stopped. He recognized the tone of voice. Scared. Keith stopped. I must have looked comical or in great danger because they both stared at me for some time while I slipped inch by inch toward falling.

The fall would not be too serious. But it was still a fall and I have never liked falling. I clamped my muscles against the rock, and the words came out of my mouth, "I can't. I'm gonna fall."

"Get onto your side," Keith said quickly. "Get your foot down lower."

"Nothing down there," I groaned, then let out a slew of obscenities between gritted teeth. I said, "Falling," but did not fall. I held on to anything I could, like trying to hang on to a glass surface.

Irvin dropped his pack and scrambled to the creek below me. He was thinking he could help, stretching up to support my boot, but he was far from reach. Keith said, "Irvin's got you," and I heard Irvin say, "What?" I thought what the hell does that mean,

Irvin's got me? That was the last of my rational thoughts and one last time I shouted, "Falling."

The rock moved past my face, grating across my lips as I fell, sliding across my chest, my thighs. I gained speed. Then, the space of the fall and the sudden impact with Irvin below. Once I hit him, I shoved him and myself into the creek, and my face took a solid smack, teeth-first, into the granite.

We lay tangled for about half a minute. Keith came and pried us off each other. I reached into the water and collected two pens launched from my shirt pocket and two buttons that had popped off. Irvin had, indeed, cushioned my fall, but had also rammed me into the rock. There was laughing, joking, but I was feeling pains around my body, feeling the nervous hammering of muscles.

We each have different coping mechanisms for dealing with our own injuries. Keith laughs like a madman. Irvin makes animated, upbeat small talk. I grow quiet and easily irritated. I was sullen for a couple more hours. I had shaken my balance. Ribs felt like they were about to pop out of my chest.

From there the granite carved into more advanced, difficult labyrinths. Along certain passageways the entire creek became a deep flume a foot and a half wide. Cocoon chambers were scooped and scoured from the rock. In this gallery show of hydrology the first saguaro cacti, green and heavy with arms, appeared like a gateway. The desert had fully arrived.

□   □   □

Days later, in the final miles before the confluence of Canyon Creek and the Salt River, we found canyon ragweed and desert lavender woven into the granite cracks. Bristling teddybear cholla grew on the slopes. Morning troops of javelina, wild desert pigs, skirted out from under mesquites and paloverdes. The larger gorge walls, thousands of feet higher, detached into buttes and pinnacles, releasing Canyon Creek. Still, in the bottom, the granite held on, white in the morning light, the water clear, ethereal. Shallow with sand, the creek hummed and swirled.

The seasons of life had changed inside my body. Alone, I rested on a boulder in pure, hot sunlight, far beyond the dark timber and snow banks of the Mogollon Rim. I was now a desert dweller.

As I had walked from high country to desert it was not the land that I felt change. It was my emotion. Every shift in color, temperature, and plant life caused a transition in my blood, in every thought. There was, of course, the quantifiable: physical geology and botany, scientific nomenclature, laws of hydrology that now governed my father's bones. But more than anything, there was emotion. I could feel the change in the land, having for two weeks walked across one of its more striking transition zones.

Walking alone — we each found our own routes down — I arrived at the confluence among great, carved boulders. There was no banner, no fanfare. Canyon Creek flowed unguarded into the deep-voiced Salt River. Water boomed into rapids. I took off every last piece of clothing and walked into the creek along its final yards. Where waters met, a sliver of a boulder stood out. I climbed on its back and sat, bringing my knees to my chest. Next to the clean rock, my skin was pale, bloodied, scraped. But I felt that my body was perfect among boulders. I sat and listened to the changed tone, to the sheer volume of the Salt River.

The movement of a creek, cutting open the Central Highlands, connecting mountain to desert, is as simple an act as I could imagine, like a song or a story. I did not think of my father and his ashes as a traveler, ceaselessly flowing from one confluence to the next. Instead, I thought of him as a process. A story being told. I thought of him as a pool of unknown trout and the busted trunk of an alder half sticking up through the water. I thought of him as a raw, deep canyon heaped with boulders and mazes of creek passages — the canyon he had once promised me. I thought of him as the beginning and the end at once.

I whispered, "Of course I don't understand all of this, Father. I'm still alive. You're dead." I brought my head to my knees so I looked more like a boulder and less like a person. The Salt River split around me, sailing through the desert.

■   ■   ■

33

# An Elite Link
## Between Diverse Life Zones

CHAPTER 2

MOUNT GRAHAM

YOU HAVE TO SIT HERE TO UNDERSTAND THIS STORY.

You have to sit atop these island mountains in southeastern Arizona and listen to every word, read every creek, smell every scent, because the story is complicated and long. Changes in animals, plants, and landscape are so abrupt here that if you walk 100 feet, you will cross boundaries that elsewhere come every 200 miles. These same changes also might come so slowly that your patience must be measured in the hundreds of thousands of years.

This chain of island mountains rises in Mexico and extends into Arizona. Each island is a mountain, remarkably tall considering the sunken smoothness of surrounding deserts. Each stands alone, ecologically disconnected from the others, rising 8 . . . 9 . . . 10,000 feet.

There are 20 other sky-island complexes in the world, consisting of "islands" of high-elevation land so secluded that few animal or plant species can move to or from them. Among these chains, this one manifests one of the richest and most unusual natural histories. It ecologically pins together the West's Rocky Mountains and Mexico's Sierra Madre. Some ecologists consider the Southwest's sky islands one of the world's rare locations of megadiversity, comparable with Madagascar and Brazil.

To explain this, I must rely on science, so bear with me. But to understand it, I need the knowledge and observations of a good friend. I can offer statistics and biological correlations, but

without this one man, the facts are meaningless. His name is Walt Anderson, one of the foremost researchers in the sky islands of Mexico and Arizona, as well as the most skilled naturalist I have ever met — hands down.

☐   ☐   ☐

We were most of the way up Mount Graham in southeastern Arizona on a cold March night below one of the Southwest's highest summits — more than 10,700 feet. We crouched in the forest, flashlights trained on a skunk mulling over our packs. Its tail floated aloft like a flaunted feather boa.

"Should we get rid of it?" I asked.

Walt, with decades of wildlife research behind him, contemplated my question. "I don't know how one gets rid of skunks."

So we watched. The last time we saw a skunk together we were in our sleeping bags below Baboquivari Peak in southern Arizona. The creature tried to get under Walt's head, digging into the clothes he had folded as a pillow. Unsuccessful there, it came to me and pounced on my chest, perching atop my sleeping bag.

"Something about you and me and skunks," Walt said tonight.

As we watched the skunk sort through our gear, Walt mentioned that the Southwest has the greatest diversity of skunk species in North America: striped, hooded, hog-nosed, and spotted. This was a striped skunk. We waited patiently, observantly, until it finally wandered off. Which is how you get rid of a skunk.

With the curious creature gone, we packed away our gear more carefully, closing zippers so the animal would not feel invited again. We took a walk along an abandoned winter road wrapping around the western slope of Mount Graham. Bundled tight, we kept our arms tucked to our bodies, our caps pulled over our ears. A shooting star winked its way through the forest as Walt began to tell me about the moths of the sky islands. His jargon and Latin terms of scientific nomenclature flowed with the sing-song tone of a storyteller.

The opening spread, Page 34, depicts the diversity of life in the Pinaleno — also called Graham — Mountains, which rise from the desert in southeastern Arizona. Counter-clockwise from top left, are beetles, Ponderosa pine in a meadow, a moth, and a stand of yuccas in a flat below the range's western slopes.

At the northern end of the Pinalenos, opposite page, a visitor sees swaths of mountains, including the Santa Teresas on the horizon, lay across the landscape shrouded by a setting sun.

A striped skunk, left, scampers around in its continual search for food. The Southwest has more skunk species than any other area in North America.

He told me that he knows a man whose research involved a five-acre parcel in southeastern Arizona. On that piece of land, looking at only a type of moth from the *macrolepidoptera* branch, he found 950 species. After saying that, he allowed the air to quiet around us. I tried to imagine 950 kinds of moths, how their wings would be shaped differently with slight variations in patterns and colors, and how they would each have distinct chemical signatures alerting others of their own species to their presence. I thought, how many niches is that? Since no two species occupy the same niche, that is 950 discrete niches. How many different habitats in only five acres? What kind of place is this that produces such variety?

I had never spent much time in the sky islands. This was Walt's territory. He is the sky islands prophet, frequently telling me stories of his travels in these mountains. Now and then I joined him to see the land that had captured him.

We crunched through gravel. Nearly 5,000 feet below us, spotting the darkness of desert, were the spider web lights of small towns. This mountain is so sheer that the lights seemed almost directly beneath our feet. Every night cold air avalanches down. Willcox, one of the towns below, can reach daytime temperatures topping 100°F, yet at night this mountain has taken the town as low as seven below, the cold accumulating at the bottom, making the desert floor colder than the mountain itself.

We paused before a winter-bare stand of aspens. Their trunks stood gray in the dark. The scent in the air shifted from the dry smell of spruces, to the sweet, slightly acidic smell of decomposing aspen leaves. Walt shuffled his hands deeper into his pockets.

"You know, I've been in the meadows just above here," he said. "At first I couldn't figure it out. I was reminded so much of Alaska. My mind kept coming back to the place. Then I realized that this is the last southern biological connection to Alaska."

When the climate alters too much toward the drier and hotter, this place becomes less and less like Alaska. Certain organisms pinch right off the top of the mountain, going regionally or globally extinct. The Mount Graham red squirrel,

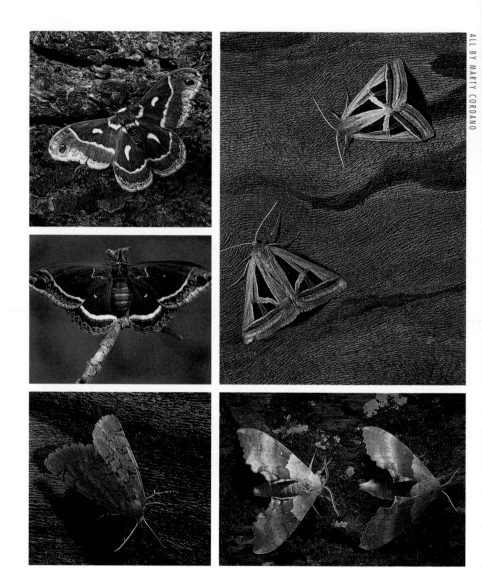

A researcher once identified 950 species of moths on a five-acre parcel in southeastern Arizona. At right are some of them featuring geometric designs and pronounced colors that serve to scare predators.

A stand of aspen trees, opposite page, serves as a reminder that the Mount Graham sky island has a biological link to Alaska and other states of the Rocky Mountains.

which exists nowhere else, now ranks among them, down to a population in the low hundreds. The last of the red squirrels are barely hanging on to the highest elevations as the climate warms (and as humans build roads and introduce competitor squirrel species for hunting), reducing its final habitat bit by bit.

What is unusual about the Southwest's sky islands is that they are the bridges between different hemispheres of the globe. So plants and animals from both north and south mingle here. Mount Graham, the tallest sky island peak at 10,720 feet, has nearly a planet's worth of environments from its base to its

In this Mount Graham scene, the oak trees in the foreground have reached the edge of their life zone, and large pine trees begin to populate the slopes as the elevation increases.

41

MARTY CORDANO

Here it is, *Tamiasciurus hudsonicus grahamensis,* the famed Mount Graham red squirrel. It lives no-where else in the world.

his own place to sleep, and we crawled into our bags, cheeks cold to the air.

◻ ◻ ◻

In the morning, I wandered alone among trees, striding slowly beneath bird call and the drum roll of woodpeckers. From my boots came the crisp breaking of weathered snow. Ribbons of sunlight worked through the spruces.

This is as dense and diverse a forest as I had seen anywhere in Arizona, easily comparable to the cool, high Kaibab Plateau north of the Grand Canyon, or the creek-riddled White Mountains along the Arizona-New Mexico border. Stout trunks stood from the snow, their climbing carpets of moss frozen. The species richness of these sky islands is unheard of elsewhere in this part of the world. Over 2,000 plant species occupy the scattered peaks. Thick-billed parrots were — before widespread hunting — residents in these Arizona pine forests.

The day before, Walt and I had walked along a creek at lower elevation, midway up the mountainside. Water splashed through a cool forest of boxelder, big-tooth maple, Arizona alder, choke-cherry, sycamore, and Arizona walnut trees. On the ground grew raspberries, shelves of fungus and moss, scouring rushes, and lush, soft-leaved meadow rue. As soon as we left the creek, entering the forests above, the world went from the likes of Mexican blue oak and netleaf oak to overlapping pines. Easily, the pines could have each been called ponderosa pine with their jigsaw puzzle bark and long, slender needles. Closer examination showed subtle differences. Some, like the Chihuahuan pine, carry tight, dark cones. The Southwest white pine has short, feathery needles. The needles on the Arizona pine droop mournfully.

As I walked across the high-elevation snow this

ALDER LEAVES

summit. Out of the desert, midway up Graham, are elements of subtropical thornscrub topped by steep oak savannas, leading still higher to rich bands of deciduous forests. Piñon-juniper woodlands rise above that, leading upward toward a Madrean pine-oak woodland, yielding then to a Rocky Mountain montane environment of large pines and creeks plunging through aspen groves. In this highest alpine landscape are the heavy, drooping arms of corkbark and white fir. Forests turn heavy with Douglas fir and their gnarled humps, burls, and wind-flagged branches.

That night, after our walk, I spread my gear between crusty banks of snow and trunks of Douglas fir. Frozen just after sunset, the ground I slept on was hard as concrete. Walt found

Oak is the dominant tree in Mount Graham's middle reaches between the desert and the peaks.

Mount Graham provides the environment for a rich assortment of birds. The spotted owl, far right, seeks out shaded canyons and fir forests with cliffs nearby. The acorn woodpecker, distinguished by a red tuft on its head, needs oak trees for acorns and pine trees in which to store them. The white-breasted nuthatch, middle, likes to hang around cottonwoods strewn along the streams of Mount Graham's lower elevations. The Arizona, or Mexican, jay is a common sight in oak woodlands.

morning, I reminded myself that only yesterday, a couple thousand feet lower, there was running water where the morning would not bring even a frost. I reached down and snapped off grass heads caked in ice.

A SMALL PIÑON

Briefly, the forest opened at an overlook, and I could see beyond Mount Graham and its string of ridges. The desert spread far below, a land of mesquite, ocotillo, prickly pear, cholla, and soap tree yucca. Standing out of the hot, dry land were other sky island mountains: the Dragoons, Swiss Helms, Dos Cabezas, the Winchesters, the Chiricahuas, the Galiuros. Corridors of greenery came down their canyons, dark tendrils moving toward the desert, but fading across the parched land. Once, 10,000 years ago, the tendrils met during a cooler climate, and the mountains were joined organically. Species were able to travel from one to the next. Now the mountains are apart.

Arranged loosely around each other, leaving plenty of space between themselves, the mountains stood like an unalarmed herd of animals. In fact, the mountains looked as if they were migrating, rumbling northward at a pace inconceivable to the human mind.

I came across Walt, who was stepping carefully to avoid breaking through the snow. He also was listening to birds. We walked together and talked. I chided him. I told him he had to produce something for the rest of us to read. The last couple years he had been working on a sky islands book for the Smithsonian Institution, but he hardly is coming closer to writing it. He incessantly roams Mexican and Arizona wildernesses, filling his file cabinets at home with notes and papers and bird lists and interviews and plant lists and field sketches. Whenever he begins to write, he feels he does not have enough information. Species are moving. Climates are changing. If he sits at home writing, he will miss the most recent transitions.

We stopped. He heard the call of a bird. He can identify not only species, but subspecies as well, by the call alone. He said, "Ruby-crowned kinglet," his eyes darting to find it.

"I don't see anything," I said.

"No. You can just hear it. Hold on," he said, and he began a bird call with his own mouth; two short, alto-pitched notes. Then two more. And two more after that. The ruby-crowned kinglet fluttered up and landed on a spruce branch 10 feet away, tittering quizzically at us.

"There we go," he said. "Now you can see it."

"What was the call you made?" I asked.

"Pigmy-owl. One of its main predators. It comes to get a closer look. I had 18 species of birds come in to me in the Chiricahuas when I was doing that. Eighteen. It was really amazing."

He pulled out his pocket notebook and wrote "RCKI" for ruby-crowned kinglet.

We walked along a narrow, forested ridge. Many of the trees had spiral fractures, the mark of lightning. Bark and shafts of wood littered the ground from the bursts of electricity. Walt touched the trees, his fingers moving slowly as if exploring the scars in a person's flesh. He is a sensual man, his voice often turning soft and curious.

At Prescott College in Arizona, he is a professor of field sciences. Students fawn over him. I was one of his students once, doing my master's work in the dynamics of water in the desert. He took weeks with me in the field, wandering canyons, chasing flash floods. In my 460-page thesis, he found commas out of place in my bibliography. His attention to detail is beyond my capacity to fathom. Sometimes I go walking with him just to listen to his voice. There are times that I do not follow his stories or his explanations. I am only lulled and enchanted by his tones.

Once, in a canyon along the U.S.-Mexico border, I was taking copious notes beside him. He turned to me and smiled.

"You're writing about the changes in geology and plant life?"

I did not stop writing as he asked his question. I had been

45

Once the site of a
military medical facility,
Hospital Flat on Mount
Graham now is a
pleasant meadow
framed by a pine
forest. The flowering
plants in the foreground
are sneezeweed.

47

Only a few miles from
scrub plants and cactus
of the Sonoran and
Chihuahuan deserts,
Hospital Flat near the
top of Mount Graham
displays its riparian
wonders, including a bit
of bluebell and yellow
monkey flowers in the
foreground and
sneezeweed in the
background.

writing about his gestures and words, not about plants and rocks. Not answering him, letting him believe I was a scientist taking notes, the next thing I penned was: "He turned to me and smiled, 'You're writing about the changes in geology and plant life?' "

He told me of fighting in the Vietnam War. His artillery battery launched mortars at men they could not see.

I asked him if it was horrible. His eyes left me for someplace else.

"It was incredible, even considering the fighting," he said. "I've never seen birds like those in Vietnam. It was such a rare opportunity."

□   □   □

Below us by 20 feet, chipmunks chased each other, screeching and tumbling in play, or in tests of dominance. Walt pulled his binoculars and watched them.

"Chipmunks really illustrate the incredible adaptive radiation of the West," he said, not taking down his binoculars.

BOTH BY MARTY CORDANO

MEXICAN
BLUE OAK

"We've got 15 or 16 species of chipmunk in the West and they've got one in the East. It shows that the West is topographical and climatically and vegetatively more island-like than the East."

"When were they last stranded here on this island?" I asked.

"Ten thousand years ago," he answered, continuing to study the chipmunks through his binoculars.

"So this line of chipmunks here has not been off this mountain for 10,000 years?" I asked.

He lowered his binoculars and thought.

"Probably not."

"How long does it take for a species in isolation to speciate (evolve into another distinct species)?"

"Generally longer than that. It can happen rapidly, but the circumstances have to be right. In the sky islands, the tide comes in and out so rapidly in evolutionary time that they haven't been isolated as long as one would like for maximum speciation. So they get overrun again by new genetic material from the same species, or they get wiped off the top of the mountain: extinction. There is just too much change here. Every time the climate changes and you get a reconnection between mountains and a re-invasion of species, you get gene swamping."

"Has anything speciated here in the last 10,000 years?"

"Not that I know of. Nothing major, at least. Just some plants and invertebrates. It would have to happen pretty quickly. We've got quite a few sub-species in the sky islands. Even some of the specialists (which live in a limited area) you find only in the sky islands, like the ridge-nosed rattlesnake. You have one race in the Animas and Peloncillo mountains and Sierra San Luis. As soon as you get over the Huachuca Mountains you have a different race of ridge-nosed rattlesnake. That also gives you

A sub-species of ridge-nosed rattlesnake lives only in places such as Mount Graham. The chipmunk comes from a line that may have stayed on Mount Graham for the past 10,000 years. Typifying diversity, chipmunks in the West fall into 15 or 16 species, while in the East there is only one.

kind of an indication of where the natural connections have been. You see which mountain ranges have a sub-species, which ones have a different subspecies. That is all in the process of these animals becoming a different species. And I think we probably have more species out here than we recognize. Mobile animals like birds won't speciate that quickly, because they're always reintroducing genes."

"But snakes have a long way to go?" I proposed.

"Perhaps," he said. "By some species definitions, different 'races' might actually be full species because they are on separate evolutionary trajectories."

In the last century, 39 mammal and bird species in Arizona and New Mexico either have vanished or been subjected to severely reduced habitats. Wolves, grizzlies, and black-footed ferrets are gone. Even elk disappeared from Arizona at one point but were reintroduced for hunting.

Curiously, as far as birds and mammals are concerned, biodiversity in the Southwest is now greater than it was in the late 1800s. While the 39 species have been cut back, 55 species have expanded their territories. The reasons are difficult to trace. Livestock grazing has been greatly reduced compared to past periods of extreme devastation. Wilderness is in better condition. Exotic species such as the black rat have spread. Climates have changed.

Some levels of disturbance can actually increase diversity. Irrigation in the Sulphur Springs Valley below Mount Graham has created ideal pocket gopher habitat that, in turn, supports the rare ferruginous hawk in good numbers. And cranes prefer the agricultural lands to native grasslands. Sewage ponds at the town of Willcox favor species that may have never been present under more pristine conditions.

The sky islands are a perfect place to find out what has come and what has gone. They are repositories of life and stepping stones for migration.

Because of the harshness of the Southwest's environment, there is little extra soil moisture or organic material to shield against climatic extremes. The sky islands, with their variety of

Post Creek in the Pinaleno Mountains flows from a montane to desert setting. It slices through a pine forest, and midway down the mountain it splashes through a cool forest of box-elder, big-tooth maple, Arizona alder, choke-cherry, sycamore, and Arizona walnut trees. On or near its banks are raspberries, fungus and moss, scouring rushes, and lush, soft-leaved meadow rue.

ALL BY DAVID W. LAZAROFF

Indian paintbrush, left,
bluebells, and verbena
thrive in the water-rich
Hospital Flat area of
Mount Graham.

climates, act like refuges, housing organisms that would have
long since disappeared.

They also act as new zones for colonization. One of the
animals officially considered gone from Arizona in the 1900s was
the jaguar. This cat boldly moved back into some of the sky
islands of the U.S. — with no help from humans — just before
the 21st century.

What is curious about animals' range expansion into the
American Southwest is that they came from the south. For the
most part they are ecologically based in Mexico's Sierra Madre.
None of the species that expanded into the sky islands is from
the Great Basin to the north, and only two — birds — are from
the Rocky Mountains, again, to the north. This is likely a sign
of species rebounding after the glacial retreat following the last
ice age.

Based on this evidence, we might conclude that the planet is
getting warmer, and species are moving to the north, leap-
frogging across the sky islands. But, truth be told, climates have
been routinely unstable and difficult to categorize since the last
ice age, 10,000 years ago. Our recent scientific observations are

almost meaningless when put in the context of time. These days,
there is much talk about strange weather and rising summer and
winter temperatures, but in the last 100 years there have been
few obvious trends in precipitation and temperature.

Regionally, some patterns have arisen. Arctic ice has begun
to melt. Snowfall has decreased in the southern Rockies. In the
past 40 years, the southwestern deserts of Arizona have warmed
significantly, but the same has not occurred in surrounding
regions. But 40 years is hardly enough to warrant any
conclusion.

I have been working on a two-million-year-old site in
Colorado, excavating Pleistocene animal bones from a cave. In
this single dig, we have discovered evidence of at least 17
different ice ages. There is no doubt that the earth's climates are
constantly tumbling over each other.

As an example of recent change, the heaviest Southwest
drought in the past 400 years occurred between 1942 and 1957,
dramatically reducing the high-elevation forests of the sky
islands. That was followed by extraordinary tree growth in the
mid-1970s, during one of the wettest series of years in the last

A dry, rocky setting on the mountain's western slopes, also has a flowering element.

53

Languishing below
Mount Graham, a
desert transition area
displays yucca plants,
which are common to
the Chihuahuan Desert.

the
Southwest's
Contrary
Land

millennia. Change can occur in very short periods.

Walt told me something. It may sound trivial or irrelevant, but it speaks directly to this changing landscape. He said that since 1971, the Mexican jay — common in the sky islands — has moved its breeding season 10 days earlier toward winter. This is not a casual shift, considering the clockwork lives of birds. Northward trends have been made clear by the expanding ranges of birds such as flycatchers, warblers, hummingbirds, even the tropical trogons. This is proof enough that the environment is changing.

□   □   □

In the afternoon we walked a road toward the summit of a lesser peak just below Mount Graham. Dry husks of cow parsnip and corn lily stood from snow banks. Snow melted under the direct sun, sending streams across open, steep ground. The ditch running along the road, against the slope, was a creek of flowing mud. Pebbles turned over themselves to get downstream. When my boot went in, the ground oozed around it like a rotten squash.

At the top of this peak, 10,028 feet, stands a fire lookout tower. Built by the Civilian Conservation Corps in 1933, the tower adds 99 feet and nine inches to the peak. Without pausing, Walt walked straight to the stairs and began climbing narrow wooden steps, hands on both rails. I followed him, making tight turns up through the steel interior of the tower, neither looking up nor down, in order to keep my balance. I noticed the brand name stenciled onto the steel: *Aermotor*, makers of windmills. Wind howled through the structure.

I stopped behind Walt on a wooden platform and looked out. Elevated above the summit, I could see clearly how this mountain teetered almost precariously atop the surrounding landscape, poking straight out of smooth earth. New Mexico came visible to the east, Mexico to the south, and the steeple of Baboquivari to the west. I could discern the full arrangement of Arizona's sky islands spread over thousands of square miles. Each of their dark, shaggy peaks stood from the desert. Streamers of lush vegetation flowed from them into pale, dry land. These

paths of life looked like roots, like bloodlines, corridors of travel that open and close over thousands and tens of thousands of years. The mountains seemed to want to touch each other, to communicate via the language of migrating organisms, but they could not.

A steely scream of wind came through the bars and cables and bolt heads of the fire tower. In the blare, Walt somehow heard the call of a bird far below us. Fighting the wind with his voice, he said, "Brown creeper." He pulled out his pocket notebook, clamping the fluttering pages between fingers. He wrote the name down, "BRCR."

How can he do this? I thought. How can he keep track of such subtle things? How can he know what is going on when at the same time I am blinded by such immensity?

Walt turned to me, the wind cutting around him, swirling against me. In his eyes I could see thousands of species, millions of years, forest fires, and droughts. I was looking into the eyes of a prophet.

"Nice view," he said.

"Yes," I replied.

■   ■   ■

# Melding Human
## and Natural Landscapes

I SAT, LEANING AGAINST ONE OF THE FENCE POSTS,

RANDY PRENTICE

letting my backpack slump to the ground beneath the boundary sign. It was a June day. Hot. The fence had been repaired numerous times, bolstered with new wire. A few posts had been added decades ago. Some of it was the original drift fence set in 1917 by rancher Freddie Fritz, Sr., who was trying to keep his Arizona cows out of New Mexico.

I was on my way to a minor creek called the Little Blue, walking out of the forested high country near the town of Alpine to the dry, woody, piñon-juniper lands far below. Alpine was the starting point because I had been a child there. I had lived near the dirt road that paralleled another stream, the Blue River, a half-hour's walk from Luna Lake, where there is a bar sometimes open and sometimes boarded up.

On my walk through this country, I had passed down from dark forests in search of the desert below. Now I was in and out of oak groves and ponderosa forests. I finished my rest and stood from the state line, hiking west, toward the coming dark of evening.

By nightfall I reached the top of a mesa beneath a shield of stars. The view from this aerie rendered a clean, absolute sweep of the universe. Constellations had no room to breathe, giving off enough light to show me to a sagebrush flat. That was where I dropped my pack and spread my gear. I sat for a while on my sleeping bag thinking back to a vivid third-grade summer spent around Alpine.

What I remembered were the raspberries. August raspberries. My mother and I used to journey into the mountains, to areas known by few people, where raspberries grew like madness. We filled buckets and gallon milk jugs with the tops cut open. Then we brought them home and stewed them for hours, spiders and all, making some of the best raspberry jam ever to be smeared on a piece of bread. Or even eaten right out of the jar with a butter knife.

Besides the raspberries, I remembered the haggard barns and corrals of surrendered ranches. I would roam through their creaking stalls and doors as if they were abandoned temples. I remembered a horse tethered in a front yard and men wearing work-polished leather gloves. I remembered marshy meadows so thick with sedges that I could reach down and grab frogs with my bare hands. I used to wander into the bracken ferns tucked in aspen groves and crouch, pretending I was in a jungle. I would climb over the slender, gray trunks of fallen aspens and climb among the standing ones, powdering my palms with the white of aspen bark. The dizzying towers of aspens used to surround me, sending me falling to my back. The aspen eyes kept watch over me by the thousands.

Now, lying in my sleeping bag, I thought it would have been far easier to remain in the aspen groves than to grow up and walk all the way down here. I thought of the liquid shade below the aspens and the quickening sound of a breeze through their heart-shaped leaves. But I have learned that land cannot be defined by a single territory. The lush, timber-filled highlands are part of a network of environments. They are not lone-standing islands. Rather, they are like water colors, with paints and tones running into each other, dripping and bleeding. To spend my time around Alpine alone would be to enforce artificial boundaries. As a child along the upper reaches of the Blue River I knew of nothing but mountains and meadows. I came on this walk to mature, to seek the meaning of land in its fullness.

☐ ☐ ☐

The high country here is called the Blue Range. The waterway coursing down the middle of the range is called the Blue River.

The opening spread, Page 56, shows some of the human and natural features of the Blue Range in eastern Arizona. The natural scenes are a stunning alpine meadow, top, and a medly of flowers in a forest. Man's signs include a post office and artwork etched into rock by prehistoric people.

Near the community of Blue, ranchers built a corral, opposite page, in a meadow at the base of a cliff.

The view from Blue Point, left, takes in an overview of the Blue Range Primitive Area in the Apache National Forest. As author Craig Childs describes it, the cleavage between landforms is dark, hiding hairpin canyons and fresh plunge holes down along the creeks. And it hides the family histories and the grizzlies and the cattle.

59

Rolling grassland meets
its boundary, slopes
covered with blue
spruce and Douglas fir
in a land of deep
wrinkles and folds.

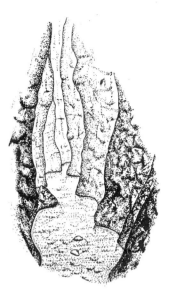

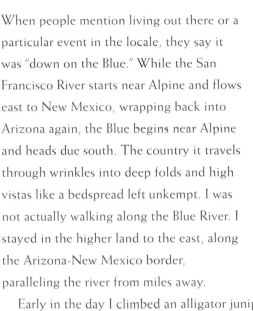

LITTLE BLUE CREEK

When people mention living out there or a particular event in the locale, they say it was "down on the Blue." While the San Francisco River starts near Alpine and flows east to New Mexico, wrapping back into Arizona again, the Blue begins near Alpine and heads due south. The country it travels through wrinkles into deep folds and high vistas like a bedspread left unkempt. I was not actually walking along the Blue River. I stayed in the higher land to the east, along the Arizona-New Mexico border, paralleling the river from miles away.

Early in the day I climbed an alligator juniper tree. I carried up through its branches a compass and a map. The tree had died more than a decade ago, but was still strong, as junipers tend to be long after death. It had the texture and color of an old woman's hair, smooth and gray. I took handholds in branches intricate like the silver work of a squash blossom necklace. I sat in the crotch of a large, motherly branch. The world below was an inlaid work of mountains, mesas, and canyons. The canyons dug around the landforms, dropping through climatic zones to the scrubby, high desert of far eastern Arizona.

Headwater mountains rose like whales over the horizons, circling the desert and spewing arrays of creeks jammed with wet thickets and meadows. Crook Creek, Flash Creek, Bear Wallow Creek, Stinky Creek, Sun Creek, Moon Creek, Paradise Creek. Below them was dry, difficult country. From high in the tree I stretched my hand out and peered straight down my forearm. I spread my fingers so that my hand covered the region where I was heading, an expanse that could envelop New York City, Seattle, or Albuquerque. The population here consists of crows, ringtail cats, scorpions, and black bears coming down for creek water. Occasionally there is a mountain lion.

I decided to leave for this low country, to get down there for a few days' taste of heat and rock. The rest of the day I climbed into the crooked canyons, loose stone, mountainsides, buttes,

Lush, timber-filled
highlands are part of a
network of zones. Their
elements — trees,
grasses, flowers, and
water — are like
colors and shapes
running into each other,
dripping and bleeding.

63

BOB AND SUZANNE CLEMENZ

and thick brush I had seen from the juniper tree. Big pines gave way to piñons and one-seed junipers, and to topsoil as dry as cracked peppercorn. Then came the thick wood of manzanitas that rake the shins and beat the knee caps. Mountain mahogany followed, and prickly pear cactus, narrowleaf yuccas. Bones of lost cows rested in the rocky, steep notches. The temperature was easily in the high 90s.

The low country was riddled with abrupt drops and vertical slots. I came to an edge where I could look to the lowest canyon floor, into a tight forest of sycamores and alders thriving off of a creek. I could hear water inside the forest. Flowing water. I found a small stream surrounded by a mob of plants and carried what I needed to the water's edge — my stove, a bag of rice and beans, empty water bottles, a small pot, and my journal. There I moved slowly into the necessary tasks, drinking first. Liquid ran down the inside of my body, cold against my throat and chest. The cables of internal muscles seized, then relaxed. I ran my bare feet into the stream.

At the creek, spiders hung from trapeze nets stretched across the water. There were so many spiders, working so diligently, that within half an hour they had me hemmed in. At dusk I climbed over them, posing awkwardly so I didn't trip the new

webs. I slept at arm's-length from the water, cradled by a nest of tree roots.

□   □   □

Long past sunrise, light and shade came down in spoonfuls. I had slept hard, as if the night had never happened. No dreams that I could remember. My head was clear. I rolled from my bag and sat up between the folded arms of alder roots. Spider webs snapped from my shoulders and floated to the ground.

Two worlds here: the canyon floor and 20 feet beyond. The floor is derived from a corridor of pools, roots, fallen trunks, spider webs, branches, trees, and damselflies. Just beyond that, for miles, for weeks, for months, are rock and banana yucca and cholla cactus.

I gathered my gear and walked into the dry country.

In the exposed roots of a juniper, I found a spear tip carved from white stone. Where it lay, it happened to point due north. The edge could still cut meat, the tip could still pierce a heart. Who knows how old? There were Mogollon people here 1,000 years ago and the Apaches in more recent times. Probably older than the Mogollons, though. It was a hunter's weapon. Big-game hunter. I picked it up, thumbed the edges, held it to the sky so light fused into its heart.

Minerals left a thin, pink vein in this translucent white stone, a good stone with fine detail etched not only by the tool work but also by the mineral hues and patterns. Someone had selected it for its strength and preciousness. I sat with my journal on my lap, making a sketch of the stone. I returned it and nudged it so that it aimed north again. When I came across a nearby arrowhead, a small, obsidian point, I did the same: Held it to the sky, then drew it.

I followed mesas that went

Blue Range country extends from conifer forests and high mountain meadows, opposite page, to a lower area festooned in places, left, with spider webs.

TWO STONE TOOLS

65

Water settled into a small basin creates a marshy wonderland. Author Craig Childs remembers such places, so thick with sedges that he could reach down and grab frogs.

The human and natural landscapes never are separable. They influence each other the way rain influences the ground. Three buildings, at right, came from wood taken from the land — a Forest Service cabin on Bear Mountain, the Post Office at Nutrioso, and a cabin built in the 1950s in the Blue Range Primitive Area.

And, opposite page, a corral in a mountain meadow shows ranchers have a stake in the area.

south, ridges that went east, and arroyos that went all over. I found a corral in a meadow of junipers and short, wait-a-minute bushes, which have thorns similar to those of its relative, the catclaw acacia, and provide forage to cattle and other animals. The fence wire had rusted so completely I could break it with one twist. Old deer antlers hung from the gate, telling stories of successful hunts.

In the dry grass, along with discarded horseshoes, was a lidded, glass Mason jar. Still sealed, it was full. The sun had fired it all day. Almost too hot to touch, the jar rolled quickly between my hands. I held it to the sun to see inside. Hard to tell what was in it. Raspberry jam, I thought. Thirty years old. Fifty years old.

Although I go to extremes to travel in places unfrequented by humans, I would have had to cover my eyes with my hands to ignore the arrowheads, corrals, and glass jars people leave behind. The human landscape and the landscape of rocks and wait-a-minute bushes never are separable. They influence each other the way rain influences the ground.

At one time, people and cows lived here in astounding numbers. It has been estimated that by 1900 a few hundred thousand head of cattle grazed along the Blue. Now, the ranchers have seen their livelihoods dwindle all the way down to this, an empty corral not used for 30 or 50 years, ground still cracked hard in places from overgrazing.

The first lower Blue cattle came with Freddie Fritz, Sr., who in 1885 homesteaded one of Arizona's storied ranches, the Triple X. This was before the Forest Service, before private land issues.

Cattle drives from around Alpine were grueling. The heavier bulls had to be shod for the rocky trek 50 miles south to Clifton, Arizona, the nearest place to sell livestock. There were dead-stock stories (A rancher's son rode with a cattle drive, taking his only steer. The animal died as soon as the drive reached the loading chutes, before the boy could get his pay. Just sat down and died, they said.). Later, in the 1900s, cattle were moved east to the new railroad at Magdalena, New

RANDY PRENTICE

The lower Blue Range country is riddled with drops and slots where a tight forest of sycamores and alders thrive off of the Blue River as it flows southward.

Mexico. Getting cattle to the railroad was an 11-day drive, man and horse.

Grizzly bears still roamed the Blue Range. In 1898, a grizzly attacked Fritz near the Blue River. Severely mauled and chewed up, the rancher never fully recovered from his injuries but didn't die until 18 years later.

These hardened ranchers welcomed the 1905 arrival of the Forest Service with the enthusiasm the Apaches gave the first ranchers to show up in the Blue Range. The Forest Service brought with it requirements for grazing permits, range management plans, per-head allotment charges, and then, in the 1960s, federally designated wilderness.

Freddie Fritz, Jr., who in the 1940s served as Speaker of the Arizona House of Representatives and as President of the Arizona Senate, continued to run cattle from the XXX until the middle 1970s, the rancher from nowhere rising into the hot politics of the city, returning home to feed cattle.

"I've no feud with the Forest Service," the younger Fritz was quoted in a 1967 *Arizona Republic* article. "And I don't want to start one, although I don't much appreciate it when a ranger right out of college rides with me two days and says everything I'm doing is wrong. One boy told me that, and I told him I was born in 1895 on this place and have hung on through times so hard he couldn't imagine them, and if I was doing everything wrong, I'd have been out of business long ago."

Fritz added to his commentary, "Many of us suspect that the long-range goal of the conservationists is to phase out the cattle operations on the wilderness areas, as soon as the wilderness areas are locked up. Then the picture will be complete — the wilderness won't be visited by many people, so it won't be seen. It won't produce. Not even the game herds can be harvested properly. My water developments will deteriorate and the brush will come in so thick a terrible fire is almost assured. There's your wilderness, as I see it."

These were words of a man born in 1895, five years after a census that enumerated 59,620 nonIndians in Arizona and 28,623 Indians, giving the state a total of 88,243 people, according to the *Historical Atlas of Arizona*, published in 1979. Now there are well over four million: people who want land; who want to build working-ranch houses and residential developments and golf courses; who want to run cattle and dig for gravel and oil; who want to construct roads and drive dirt bikes and go out shooting beer cans; who want to preserve watersheds; who want to find even a semblance of wilderness; who want to wear crystals, burn incense, and chant prayers to ancient deities. There are so many of us that we will chew up the place faster than 100,000 starved bovines. Not just the grass, but the rocks, and the sky.

Fritz's vision did not come to pass exactly as he thought. He could not have anticipated the sheer number of people to come.

I have bucked 20 tons of hay with ranch families, kicked slabs of it out of flatbed trucks to the waiting throngs of cattle on subzero dawns, and sipped black, hard coffee with people who know nothing but cows, fence, horses, and weather. Which, in a sense, is knowing everything. I have been astounded with the fullness of their lives. From five o'clock one morning when I walked in the dark with a ranch woman to break ice at the creek so the cattle could get to the water, to dark that night when the cattle gate was closed behind the pickup, there was work to be done. Solid work. Work that has no end because it has no beginning. There is no hiatus to the life of a cow. The seasons do not pause. Fence always needs mending.

Many times when I have worked with ranchers or talked to them, I have thought that the rest of us are expendable. I have thought please, please, let these people survive. There is something immutably good about ranchers I have known. Something so firm that I could hold it, I could smell it.

Never let these people die.

But there are places where there should be no cows, places that can hardly support deer and rodents. I have seen a good creek go bad after 20 cattle have been turned out. Turn bad for years, still bad to this day. The fish die. The creek slows as it spreads, oozing across a shoreline that has been trampled to mud and manure. The water goes warm, oxygen-poor, and sick with disease. I have seen grassland metamorphose into a lunar landscape, hospitable only to ground beetles and species of slender mushrooms that grow exclusively in animal dung.

The first cattle brought to the American West belonged to the Spaniards. That was 400 years ago, which was when things began to change.

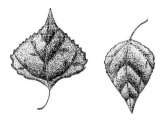

FREMONT AND NARROWLEAF
COTTONWOOD LEAVES

Over a billion acres of semiarid grassland, like what once existed in this scrub desert, has since been swept off of North America. Grasses in the desert, like black grama, once had power in numbers, but as soon as they were eaten away, they were gone for good. The land changed. Erosion increased dramatically. Species began to vanish at a rate not seen for millions of years, leaving a devastating imbalance further molested by poor land management and irrational development.

In much of the Southwest, the environment can be sustainable alongside the cattle industry only with a limited number of animals on a rotating grazing plan. And that only if no drought or flood alters the condition of the range; if the coyotes, wolves, ravens, and eagles don't get shot, poisoned, and trapped by those defending livestock; if the cattle somehow stop wallowing along creeks, turning them into swamps; if piñon and juniper forests don't get toppled by bulldozers to open land for grazing; and if grasses are not chewed to the hilt by livestock until they can't hold the soil any longer.

And, honestly, I do not know how to weigh these requirements against the life of ranchers. So much pressure goes against them: the wind, the calves born in blizzards, the rogue cow broken from a cattle drive (running reckless for miles chased by a screaming cowboy), and the rain — the hours, days, and weeks of rain. Add to that pressures from conservationists.

I tell you though, things will never get easier than this. The land has always been complex and, in turn, humans have always been enigmatic.

An Arizona rancher named Toles Cosper once ran cattle down

71

A rocky floor and prickly pear plants clinging to a cliff, right, show that the Blue River has completed its run from mountain to desert.

lures and cork bobbers. My grandmothers and great-grandmothers made complimentary, protocol words toward the catches. They fried them in butter on iron skillets, battered with nothing but cornmeal and salt. The trout were so fresh that they curled like leaves when they hit the pan. We would have picnics up there. Drop a blanket, gather raspberries at places like Crows Poison, catch fish out of the Blue, the White, the Black, and Luna Lake.

But down here, where most of the creeks have gone dry, life is different. A different paradise. A different hell. You can't bask in the warm, pine tree bliss with sounds of giggling, chortling creeks putting you to sleep. Here it is hard, sharp, and hot. At the same time, it is more pure, more refined. Aspects are brought down to fundamental levels: rock, sky, bone.

In the early evening I found bear tracks in sand. They were somewhat fresh, a couple days old. I held my hand over one of the prints, careful not to set it down and disturb the sand. My hand was larger. It was a young black bear, traveling unusually low in elevation for this time of the year. Probably it was on its way from one cool place to the next, taking a short cut through the desert. I stood and smelled the air, lifting my head to the darkening sky.

The last known grizzly here is believed to have been killed in 1935. Before that, ranchers reported grizzlies constantly. It was not the mountain lions, the coyotes, or the Mexican wolves that raised the ranchers' greatest ire. It was the grizzlies. They feasted on calves in the spring, and then, before hibernation, in early winter.

Certain animals that have been driven out of the West by humans are slowly being returned. With migratory routes severed and with a vehement lack of local interest, reintroduction is a difficult task. In April of 1998 the area around the Blue was the target of the first Mexican wolf reintroduction. Eleven wolves were brought in, and before the year was over five had been shot and killed. Another has never been found, its fate presumed the same. Those that survived were captured by U.S. Fish and Wildlife agents and taken to New Mexico in search of a warmer welcome.

RANDY PRENTICE

Nearby, not far from what now is a campground, a rock surface bears the mark of a prehistoric people, probably members of the Mogollon Culture who were in the area until around A.D. 1400. The Mogollon sometimes are called the first mountain farmers of the Southwest.

75

There has been talk of bringing the grizzly back as well, but if the wolf reception can be taken as an indicator, the bears would likely be met with guns.

Why bring them back?

Some arguments suggest that they are part of an intricate wildlife check and balance, and if they could somehow find their way in, then they would prosper.

Why keep them out?

Because humans have charged themselves with the godly role of managing the planet and, suspiciously, we have a bias dictating which species we want to see and which we don't.

Between grizzly bears and ranch families, the last hundred years down on the Blue have seen as many transitions as the land offers between mountain and desert. The land went from forest to dry scrub and back, from creek to dust to creek. As if following suit, ranch communities rose and fell, wilderness gave way to range land, which fell back to wilderness. Amid this, the Mexican wolf and the grizzly vanished. This place seems to invite transformation.

□   □   □

Little Blue Creek flows through slots and narrows several miles above its confluence with the Blue River. When I finally arrived, the air was well past 100°F. I glided through cool, running creek water to my waist. The creek broke across rocks in a clatter of white noise. I walked into a hollowed undercut where I could drag my fingertips across the ceiling. In the back was a mudded nest adhered to the wall, hanging over the water. I waded to it and stood on my toes. With my eyes against the lip of the nest I could see in it a pink ball with a bit of gray fuzz. I clucked my tongue and the ball disassembled itself into three newborn chicks, mouths wide open. The parents, a pair of northern rough-winged swallows, zig-zagged through the canyon, chattering at me. They darted in my face as I walked out.

Ahead were holes so deep that I could not cross without swimming. I took my pack up into the cliffs and skirted around. One pool's bottom projected an inviting, oak barrel darkness. I set my pack on a ledge, following it with my boots and my clothes. I then crept naked to the edge, looking 25 feet down into the well.

Before I knew it, before I even gave the order, I jumped. No grace or art. I was a flailing body, arms and legs kicking. I plunked into the water and swam down until my ears hurt. When my hand touched sand I swung around and kicked my way to the surface. I climbed back to my gear and dried off.

From here I planned to hike into New Mexico again, leaving the creek for the dry piñon-juniper woodlands beyond, and the ponderosa forests of Maple Mountain beyond that. I filled water bottles with as much as I might need. One gallon. In the brass sun of late afternoon I hiked southeast, high out of the canyons and valleys.

At sunset I mopped sweaty bangs out of my eyes. To the northwest herds of thunder clouds turned shadowy as they broke apart. The day was over. The heat was off.

I could easily see down to where I had been walking for the past several days. Red sunlight bent to the horizon like an arc of polished cherry wood. Long, round mountains nested into each others' backs. Where they met they sent out mesas and buttes. The cleavage between landforms was dark. The darkness hid its hairpin canyons and fresh plunge holes down along the creeks. It hid the family histories and the grizzlies and the cattle long gone. So much is held by a piece of land. What amazes me, though, is that I can walk away from it. I can climb up the side of a mountain and turn back to see that it is just some piece of acreage, perhaps no different than the one I could see to the east, or to the south. Stories are absorbed so easily by distance that you might never know what is out there.

■   ■   ■

Hoodoo formations tower over pine trees in Blue Range country in the Apache National Forest.

# A Gathering Place
## for People and Geography

THE ASSIGNMENT CAME ON A PAY PHONE. SEDONA.

BOB AND SUZANNE CLEMENZ

I leaned against the phone booth, tapping the butt of a pen against my head.

Go to Sedona, my editor instructed, and write about the immense variety of landscape bundled up in a area a person could travel over in a day. He cited rock monoliths with names like Cathedral Rock and Giant's Thumb; a rust-toned desert that once was a sea; rugged, rocky canyons, and the verdant, watery splendor of Oak Creek.

I suggested that our purpose might be served if I ventured to other regions, some unnamed canyons far from Sedona that would remain unnamed, places that represented dramatic environmental transitions just as Sedona does.

My editor insisted, "Do Sedona. You've already got all of these other places that you wanted. I'd like to hear your observations about Sedona."

Our exchange was over. I hung up.

Damn.

The area, interchangeably referred to as Sedona and red rock country, reigns as one of the most spectacular road-and trail-accessed landscapes known to humankind. Within 10 miles of Sedona the town, seven of Nature's communities thrive, ranging from cactus- and grass-laced desert, to water-rich strips with oak and maple trees, grasses, and ferns, to pine and fir forests on mountainsides and tops. Here, explosive and

ever-changing colors bathe monoliths and chiseled cliffs.

Sedona sits below the southwestern edge of the Colorado Plateau, a landmass covering approximately 130,000 square miles spread over parts of four states. Here, the massive plateau crumbles down to its final canyons and toppling stone pillars. The town creeps up through this boundary, sending some of its churches and luxury homes into the cracks in the bottoms of cliffs.

Despite this natural bounty, the place poses as my nemesis: gridlock tourism, unrestrained expressions of wealth, the sound-byte industry of enchantment and mysticism, and the parasitic use of wild lands. For this, Sedona evokes mourning from me. I have accepted it as a sacrificial land, stunning to the eye but wholly given over to humanity — to be consumed like flesh among piranhas.

Not to sound grim, I promised my editor I would write nothing of the sort, but instead would focus on the land's assortment of natural treasures.

But how could I ignore humanity's incursion? I had a friend who managed a Sedona convenience store, and from behind the counter, along with Marlboros and sun visors, he dispensed daily directions to New Age spiritual centers of the universe easily accessed by foot trails.

About this new destination I complained bitterly to my fiancée, Regan, a woman who has less social grace than I in the back country. Upon hearing the hikers' footsteps she tends to hide among bushes, as if that act were the normal thing to do. She expresses little love for others in the wilderness. I procrastinated in front of her, not wanting to talk about traveling to Sedona. I purchased no maps, made no plans.

Finally, she let out a huff of breath, rolled her eyes, and said, "It's land, Craig. It's a place. Try to have a little faith in it."

We arrived in town and went about the activities we reserve for civilization, looking for a laundry that takes no more than 75 cents a load and setting up a communications center at a cluster of pay phones outside a strip mall. I called everyone I needed to but my editor. I crouched against the cinder block wall and studied the throbbing traffic on the main street. Behind the cars

The opening spread, Page 78, shows some of the landscapes that always have drawn people to Sedona. Clockwise from top left are visitors touring red rock country, a home built by prehistoric people who found safety in the cliffs, a medley of fall colors mixed with evergreens along the West Fork of Oak Creek, and the sandstone ramparts of Wilson Mountain north of Sedona.

Reflected in Oak Creek, opposite page, Cathedral Rock stands as an icon for Sedona's hundreds of thousands of visitors.

Sedona, left, sends some of its churches and luxury homes into the cracks and bottoms of cliffs along the southwestern edge of the Colorado Plateau.

81

FRANK ZULLO

FRANK ZULLO

and the buildings, huge, solid sandstone monuments accelerated into the sky.

"What's going on here?" I asked, not meaning for anyone to hear.

Regan was dialing another number. She paused and spoke to me.

"This is the edge."

"What's up there?" I asked, gesturing with my chin toward the forests and cliffs.

Regan glanced up and said, "What you are looking for."

I hate it when she gets so wise and curtly articulate. That usually means I am missing the point. So, still crouched at the pay phone, I studied Sedona's northern backdrop, a giant slab of eroded sedimentary rock perched above the surrounding land. Banded walls of white and red dominate the view. The town itself, like the geography around it, hosts a meeting of vastly different origins. Difference begets difference, and the landscape has directly influenced the gathering of people.

A man living here widely claims to be a "Level Four Audio Fusion Material Compliment for an Interdimensional Being" in charge of "The Local Universe." He prophesizes that Sedona will soon be the seat of a "Divine New Order Government" whose body will include "Nefertiti, Mary Magdalene, Francis of Assisi, and the close family of Jesus, son of God." Another element, what the spiritual man might consider the occupation of lesser souls, is jet set golf. A 40-minute helicopter flight zips players from Scottsdale to Sedona for 9:30 tee times at the Sedona Golf Resort, then returns them for afternoon tee times at a golf course below the Superstition Mountains east of Phoenix. Between these extremes are the entrepreneurs and refugees surviving in an amenity-based town. I have a cousin here who works on computers. It is a place to make a living.

Demographically, the Colorado Plateau ranks as a cultural island, far different from surrounding regions. No large cities inhabit the plateau, yet Phoenix, Las Vegas, Albuquerque, and Salt Lake City lie just off each of its cardinal points. One in 10 houses on the plateau has no telephone, one in eight no

The constellations Lyra the Harp and Cygnus the Swan, opposite page, punctuate a starry mantle over the Chapel of the Cross, an inverted wedge of concrete and glass rising from Twin Buttes on Sedona's southern edge. Although it is not the site of regular services, the church is open daily to the public.

Lyra, left, and its brightest star, Vega, shine over a stand of jojoba and piñon in red rock country.

Oak Creek Canyon embraces a tame evergreen-covered expanse that falls off into rugged canyons and then resumes In the crevices and top of Wilson Mountain.

85

plumbing. A quarter of the entire landmass belongs to Native American tribes. Much of it is wilderness. These wildernesses and demographic boundaries directly hit the edges of Sedona, where almost every household has plumbing and telephones, and Native Americans are heavily represented by books, beads, and feathers-for-sale, but not by actual people.

The night Regan and I left our pay phones, we camped on the side of a dirt road. Around Sedona, the U.S. Forest Service has banned camping on much of the public land it oversees because crowds were threatening to change the nature of the land. We tried to get as far away as we could beyond the no-camping signs. Headlights kept coming by, even 15 miles out on the road. Pink Jeeps carrying tourists on backroad tours continued into the dark.

I took a night walk alone, wandering up through brush until reaching a cliff. Its surface was the texture of coarsely grained sandpaper. There I climbed and found a place to sit and study the starlit terrain. I still had the question on my mind of what exactly I was doing here in a place I've so thoughtfully avoided. I spread my hands on the sandstone upon which I sat. There is a palpable weight to having such a large landmass come to an end here under my body. This southwestern boundary of the plateau stands higher than any of its other boundaries. Everywhere to my back canyons tangled and plunged as they broke away from their sandstone platforms, dropping toward the country below.

The Colorado Plateau persists as a raft of geologic stability in this continent's upheaval. Beyond the edges, the world looks like a car accident, fenders and hoods crumpled. The Rocky Mountains to the east jam against the plateau, breathing down its neck. To the south and west, what I could see from here, lies the Basin and Range Province, a geological hazard area with blocks of earth thrust at angles. The plateau sits in the middle and breathes slowly, uplifting or falling at a relatively even rate. For over 400 million years it was a low point gathering bands of sediment, rising now and then so that erosion could scrape off a few of the top layers. It is now rising again, having gently lifted for the last 10 million years. This lift has exposed these millions of years of rock — incredible ribbons of color and cliff that have brought Sedona its fame.

Hills and mesas defined the world I looked at. Vegetation streamed out from beneath these parched, red cliffs, flowing toward the rolling horizons as if set free. Behind that the world was a garden of eroded stone forms extending for hundreds of miles.

On a geologic map with rock types distinguished by color, the Colorado Plateau is a circle of easy tones. The rest of the world looks like an angry child got to it with crayons. That is why people come to Sedona. It is the boundary between worlds. This is the place to gather. For spiritual sanctuary. For money. For a golf vacation. For contrast.

I sat beneath the weight of the Colorado Plateau, watching the headlights of another Pink Jeep tour cruise through the basin below. I stood and stepped into neck-deep stands of mountain mahogany, wading back down to Regan and the truck.

□   □   □

The next morning we walked up one of the more popular trails. Boynton Canyon. A resort called Enchantment is stuffed into the mouth of Boynton, but I must sheepishly admit that the design and construction are done with grace and a reasonable paint job rarely seen around such opulence. For an "outdoor" resort, it was not agonizingly garish.

Weeks later, out of curiosity, I would call one of the head architects who had worked on Enchantment. His name is Darrin Orndorff, and he works with an architectural firm out of Phoenix. My first question was why.

"The owners know the value of the surrounding environment," he said. "We realized what the major amenity was here, and if we didn't build with it, we'd lose the beauty that drew us here."

"What did you consciously do to create this form?" I asked.

"Low profile. Hugging the terrain. We tried to keep structures low, positioning each one so that it settles into another, not stacking up and blocking other buildings. We walked the land before doing anything so we could wrap around trees and rocks that don't show on the map."

One edge of the 130,000-square-mile Colorado Plateau, stretching across the horizon, crumbles down to its final canyons and bands of color in the Sedona area. In the foreground lies Bear Wallow Canyon.

87

GEORGE STOCKING

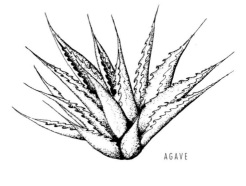

AGAVE

Most of our discussion stuck with the technicalities of building. I tried to elicit a philosophical reason for what he had done, but I wasn't getting anything. Still, I will naively believe that beneath the cost-effectiveness and the amenity there is a philosophy. Enchantment has unlit places and buildings that could have been constructed more efficiently, but weren't. People, even people with money and luxury, still crave the order of wild things. I asked why this is not done more often.

"Well, look at people's yards," he said. "One person will keep it trimmed every day. Another person lets it go a little wild. It's a difference of personality. To be honest, it is more affordable to keep it trimmed and build something that doesn't purely blend with the landscape. The laws around access for disabled people limit our ability to comply with the landscape. And we're used to a certain way of doing things. You have a staff to replace the flowers and maintain the grass. You have a budget that runs a certain way, and alternative types of architecture and landscaping are outside of that budget. And some people just don't like it. They want a place that has other amenities. Not wild places."

As Regan and I walked that morning, construction was in full swing, sending up concrete walls for a new section of Enchantment. A fleet of cement trucks and backhoes moved in and out. The sound gathered into a roar and curled high overhead in the sandstone amphitheaters. I sat and scribbled in my notebook, mentioning the variety of colors represented by hard hats. The orderly diversity seemed to suggest a pecking order. Architects, supervisors, and workers. Regan had gone ahead. She returned.

"This will blow your mind. Come just over here."

I pocketed the notebook and followed her for 15 feet. Her arm pointed toward the cliff.

"There, there, and there," she said.

Each point was a small cliff ruin. Made of stone and mortar, none was much larger than a 55-gallon drum. They had been fitted by the Sinagua Culture around 700 years ago into the cracks and eroded bedding planes of the Supai formation.

Inconspicuous, they were built of local rocks and mortar made from canyon mud. Like us, and like people staying at Enchantment, the Sinagua had come here too, right up to the edge. Directly below, a man installed a plate glass window into a newly built home. The home and the ruins were not more than 300 yards apart. I could hear the squeak as he wiped his fingerprints from the glass.

The trail between the ruins and the house runs exclusively within a federally protected wilderness area, its boundary marked by a fence. Immediately to the west of the fence were buildings and paved stairs. Wilderness and civilization rubbed shoulders so tightly there should have been heat from the friction. Instead of heat, yuccas and manzanitas grew with glossy branches squeezing through the fence.

As the trail came into the canyon floor, oaks and junipers spread to form a canopy, the ground dry, but shaded. Ruins appeared frequently among the surrounding cliffs, some large enough to have been dwellings. A matter of miles from here, in the early 90s, a passenger on a scenic helicopter tour spotted an undisturbed archaeological site in the cliffs. He reported this to the Forest Service and immediately archaeologists climbed up. In the shade of an alcove they found a gathering of gracefully rounded pots and other artifacts. The largest pot, able to hold 30 gallons, lay slightly tilted to the side, its mouth round and dark. Of course, within days of this discovery, word got out. Two baskets, a sifter made of yucca fiber, and a pot went missing. The archaeologists returned and pulled out each artifact to prevent those remaining from being stolen.

How many other places are there? I walked, looking into the surrounding cliffs. As many people had once lived in Boynton Canyon as now were paying a few hundred dollars a night to stay at Enchantment. People tended to the construction of buildings where crops of maize grew 700 years ago. The obviousness seemed startling. People always come to the same places. The

People always come to the same places, opposite page. Spotted by the sun, a house in Boynton Canyon stands out. Concealed elsewhere in the canyon are the ruins of living quarters and food-storage caches of prehistoric people.

89

High in Boynton Canyon, opposite page and left, people of the Sinagua Culture searched out sheltered areas in the cliffs to build their communities.

eyes of a helicopter tourist fall exactly where the Sinagua had found shelter and stored their pots.

The Sinagua had sought refuge here during a time of warfare and the collapse of regional pueblos. For protection they utilized cliffs that now are sought out for their staggering beauty. These were the amenities Enchantment's architect had mentioned, the amenities of safety and beauty. Refuge is taken by businesspeople and affluent travelers. Livelihoods are made by waiting tables and constructing new buildings. To walk across one of Enchantment's verandas, drink in hand, fresh towels back in the room, and see this protective canyon — this is comfort. To cultivate crops with hundreds of others, knowing there are food and protection here, dry places to sleep and complex terrain to escape into if need be — this is comfort.

Eventually the vegetation tightened as the canyon drew farther into the plateau, miles from Enchantment. Chandeliers of mistletoe hung from juniper trees. Hedgehog cacti grew among moist beds of club moss. We ran out of trail and beat back through thickets of mountain mahogany, climbing eventually to the sandstone base of one of the monuments. While I stayed below and looked across the landscape, Regan climbed 20 feet up

into a darkening crack, calling correspondence back down. She said it was a cave, that she felt wind coming out of it. I could hear her struggles, the slip of skin against rock as she climbed.

"It's got a yummy, dank smell," she reported.

I looked up to see her body fully stemmed between the walls on both sides of the formation. She could have found better footing down the middle, where clay-like mud supported a garden of liverworts. She didn't want to leave a footprint, though. It seemed futile and irrelevant, but her care was noted. No one else would ever come to this place, and she took care of it perhaps for that very reason.

"I can see water," she said. "I hear drips. Splashing. There's a pool up here."

I studied her, thought about going up, but there was only room for one. I had a good view here. Most of Boynton Canyon and its arms opened beneath me, lacing the bottom of these massive stone temples. Pretty soon her voice was muffled, reporting back like words from the moon.

"Oh! A drip down my back."

She was trying so hard not to leave footprints that it looked like she was suspended over glass. She pulled a flashlight from her pack, held it between her teeth, and wormed farther in. A few minutes later she climbed down with bare arms and shoulders painted in red mud. Mats of spider web hung from her hair. She grinned, wiped some of the mud from her arm and stroked a single finger on each cheek, applying it like blush.

I smiled back at her. She had found something. Exactly what she was looking for. An unannounced, unexpected, small discovery. I have always witnessed beauty in her for her ability to uncover secrets that would matter to few others. But I was still searching for mine.

□   □   □

The secret came the following week. A heavy March snow smothered Northern Arizona. The largest storm of the year. The morning after, as clouds snagged and tore across the earth, I drove to Sedona, and then up to the trailhead at the West Fork of Oak Creek. The place sees more than 90,000 hikers a year. I

Like a giant, Oak Creek Canyon draws a deep breath and pulls a storm from its open southern end into the relatively narrow crevice of its upper end.

93

SYCAMORE LEAF

BIG-TOOTH MAPLE LEAF

figured this would be the day I could avoid most of them. At the cold, pay-parking trailhead, I folded five one-dollar bills into a fee envelope, dropped it in the appropriate slot, and walked away from the conspicuously vacant parking lot.

The trail turned from Oak Creek and entered the high cliffs of a canyon. This was one of the many canyons crowding down to the edge of the Colorado Plateau. It did not have the warm openness of Boynton Canyon, nor did it have the placement of giant monuments. It was an intimate sliver through the bedrock, hundreds, and then thousands, of feet deep. The canyon and its creek were capped in snow. There were footprints, but after a mile they quickly pared down to random stomps in drifts and heaps of snow.

The immediate vicinity of Sedona is desert. The top of the plateau, which leads to the town of Flagstaff, is forested. The canyons dropping between are the connection points, threads of vegetation trailing down before vanishing into the desert. One of these, the West Fork of Oak Creek, is a perfect conduit, tall and narrow enough to be constantly cool or cold, filled with rare vegetation. Douglas fir outnumber ponderosa pines. Agaves and manzanita climb out of the south-facing bends. Along the canyon floor, high humidity, shaded alcoves, and springs leaking from the wall invite a floral arrangement not seen in this part of the world since the last ice age. Growing here are wild basil, thimble berry, Arizona bugbane, hop-hornbeam, red dogwood, black medic. The moist seeps dripping from canyon walls host hanging gardens of 85 plant species that grow along these sheer rock springs and nowhere else.

The seeps now were frozen into sheets. Ice had cast an enamel layer over vines and roots dangling beneath ledges. I wore gloves and two layers of warm sweaters. As I walked through knee-deep snow, dirigibles of slush and snow fell from fir

"The air seemed rarefied, the scent of winter strong," author Craig Childs writes in describing a trek into the upper reaches of the West Fork of Oak Creek Canyon, left and opposite page. Recalling an earlier hike nearby, he observes, "That such a broad, warm canyon could exist so close to here seemed impractical, like something that the land would not do."

Snow clings to the nonvertical surfaces of a sandstone palisades in the West Fork of Oak Creek Canyon north of Sedona.

branches overhead, hitting beside me or lighting into the creek where they sailed for a moment before dissolving. It was March snow. Heavy with moisture, nearly as dense as cheesecake, it kept me moving slowly. I stopped frequently to study some curiosity, scouring rushes sheathed in cylinders of ice, or a ribbon of snow crested along a fallen maple. I spent 15 minutes with a haphazard pile of twigs and half-branches that had been turned to interlocked antlers of ice.

Three miles back, the canyon closed, crimping the creek into running wall to wall. I hesitated for a moment, then went ahead, walking into the water. Instantly my boots filled. Cold, stinging water. Up to my knees. The creek ran smooth and quiet. Some of the snow above was melting, giving an offset rhythm of water dripping from a hundred feet overhead. Stopping for a moment, letting muscle cramps in my calves subside, I tilted my head back and watched the dizzy plummet of water drops.

I waded into a low passage with a curved ceiling, pushing through a shelf of ice where the surface of the creek had frozen. A puzzled trail of floating shards gathered behind me. Ornate icicles wrapped around each other over my head. Hundreds of them. Ferns and the straw of last season's monkey flowers hung between the icicles, but even they were wrapped in ice, their forms captured beneath glassy shells.

Moving steadily through a cathedral of ice and dripping melt water, I reminded myself that soon night would come. By then, only a couple hours away, I would need to be dry and far from here. But I had passed the final footprints of anyone else and was the first to come through the ice. This precious vacancy urged me forward.

When there was enough room in the canyon, I walked out of the water and onto shore. Now the snow came above my knees, and my soaked pants quickly froze around my legs. I followed the turtle-shell outlines of creek boulders far beneath the snow, taking a few seconds for each deep step. Willows had been wrestled to the ground by the weight.

Stopping at an alcove, I promised myself I would turn around here. I relinquished the next bend of the canyon to the

VEGETATION IN THE FORKS
OF OAK CREEK

coming night. Drapes of icicles guarded the front of the alcove. I ducked around them and sat in the dry back, an arm's reach from the stalactite ice. I was tempted to break one off. Just to hear the snap. To suck water out of it. But I didn't dare. Not during such a quiet, snowed-in moment. Not when I was entrusted with coming here alone. The air seemed rarefied, the scent of winter strong.

The creek flowed easily, making few noises as it followed the canyon, bubbling as it passed beneath the ice. From here it runs into Oak Creek, and Oak Creek flows a short distance to Sedona and cuts straight through town. Feeding into it also, even though dry, is Boynton Canyon. I thought back to only a week earlier when Regan and I had walked through temperatures in the 80s, the ground crisply parched. That such a broad, warm canyon could exist so close to here seemed impractical, like something that the land would not do. But land is contrary, especially where one territory meets another.

After a time of sitting, pant legs frozen stiff around my calves, I stood and walked out. The fog of my breath brushed the air as I waded through the creek. Ninety thousand people would be back. Seeking visual contrast, spiritual enlightenment, beauty, a good walk, or a family weekend outdoors, they would be back. We always return to the same places.

■ ■ ■

# Here in the Canyons
# Rock Defines Diversity

GARY LADD

to canyon, I sat with a friend alongside a dwindling fire. His face was lit pumpkin orange by embers. We had not spoken in hours, eating our meal, setting bowls aside, staring at the fire. The winter temperature came spiraling down around us. Hands ventured out of gloves every few minutes to drift toward the warmth, fingers almost touching the coals. Before the last flame went out, he looked up at me.

"What is it about this place" he asked, "that makes us seek out the deepest, darkest crevice in the ass-end of nowhere?"

Without looking at him, I thought about this, giving another couple minutes of quiet. We were on the very back edge of nowhere, not even within two days of any sort of trail. We had traveled through canyons so deep and twisted that it was easy to lose track, to become irretrievably lost. I finally just said, "Don't know."

If our fire was somehow visible from the air, from a jetliner, it would be a speck of light, a single faint star in infinite space. No cities have found purchase in this dry, hard land radiating from the Four Corners where Arizona, Colorado, New Mexico, and Utah meet. Few towns have found their way in. Highways, even those of dirt, go hundreds of miles out of the way to avoid the countless fissures and chasms. The canyon country is a difficult place in which to live. It is the perfect land.

I first came to this land at the age of 10, being introduced to

Lake Powell, on the Arizona-Utah border. A group had rented a houseboat and I came along with my father from Phoenix. I knew nothing of the dam holding back the Colorado River, or even of the fact that this was not a natural body of water. What I knew was that rising from the water were curious walls of stone where hardly a single plant or animal lived. Every time we tied the boat to land, I scurried into the rocks. I found strange stones worn like marbles, infused with peculiar colors. They were grainy, soft enough to break with a mildly hard blow. Later in life, I would learn that they came from a formation called Navajo sandstone. But when I was young, the rocks had no name. I filled my pockets and returned to the boat to unload them, then came back out and filled my pockets again. And again. The houseboat became a haphazard museum of small stones. None of the others knew who was bringing them in.

We took the houseboat into the dim, narrow corridors of drowned canyons. People stood on either side, shouting if the boat came too close to the walls. In the back of one canyon, we spent an hour puttering along, sometimes scraping the roof of the houseboat against sandstone overhangs.

One evening a storm came across Lake Powell, creeping toward us while I was on shore picking up rocks. The sun had set, the color gone. I looked up, and to the north the sky burned with an eerie light. Red. Deep, luminous, blood red. At first, I thought there must be a forest fire. Then, I realized that there were no forests. The sky had gone haywire. What a strange place, I thought, where the sky lights on fire. From the south I heard thunder. I ran onto the houseboat, announcing that the world had turned mad, my hands clutching small rocks. The men were already drinking and laughing, so I was regarded with brief suspicion and curiosity. They saw the rocks in my hands.

I went back out alone and watched. Later, I would learn that for a brief, rare instant, the aurora borealis was visible as far south as Utah. I wondered if at that moment there was no human but me out there to look at the luminous phenomenon in the sky. This was an even more enchanting thought to me than that of the aurora borealis: a land without people.

The opening spread, Page 98, helps explain author Craig Childs' point: "To understand the simplest aspects of this territory of canyons, you have to first see that no rock resembles another." Clockwise from top left are delicate fins formed by grains of sand pressed together, rock worn smooth on one side of Lake Powell and rising into buttes across the way, streaked Navajo sandstone, and the sculpted rock of the Grand Canyon.

Seen at sunset from 10,388-foot Navajo Mountain, opposite page, one arm of Lake Powell is formed by the San Juan River, itself the beneficiary of numerous streams in Colorado, New Mexico, and Utah as it flows from the Rocky Mountains across the Colorado Plateau.

Layers of sandstone, left, form Last Chance Bay in Lake Powell.

101

In this land of mostly rock, a place such as Lake Powell's Lone Rock Bay exists because of a dam across the Colorado River.

STEVE BRUNO

So Canyon Country is where I have come to spend much of my life. With my friend at the fire in Utah, I sat into the night, stirring coals with a stick as the air temperature dropped to near zero. Whatever the answer was to his question about the far end of nowhere, I had spent well over an hour pondering it. This is a land that draws me beyond imagination. Its shapes of twisted stone and juniper are not what a person should expect of the earth. As one canyon enters another, the world changes. Transitions heap atop transitions like a tangled jungle, but one made of stone rather than greenery. You can walk from Utah into Arizona, from the Waterpocket Fold to Paria Canyon to the Grand Canyon, and you will have passed through so much process and transformation that your notes make it look as if you have walked the globe. That is why I come here.

· □ · □ □

To understand the simplest aspects of this territory of canyons, you first have to see that no rock resembles another. The way it was formed hundreds of millions of years ago, the way it erodes, how it cleaves open when it falls 50 feet, how lichens might take to it — these factors all change a rock's signature. I don't mean to be esoteric here, or to rely on subtleties that an untrained eye won't see, but it's true. Each rock is remarkably unique. In a place made almost solely of rock, and of thousands upon thousands of canyons — their rocks ranging in size and number beyond the limits of mathematics — there will be no canyon that looks like the next.

The plateau itself makes up most of northern Arizona and southern Utah, and some of adjacent Colorado and New Mexico. It is an approximately 130,000-square-mile shield of uplifted stone, across which four large rivers run through massive gorges they have carved. The surrounding land is worked into canyons heading tens and hundreds of miles toward the nearest river.

The whole place is designed like the roots of a tree branching over and over again. Each canyon leads into another, and then another. The rivers in them, in fact, consume each other. The Yampa River joins another and becomes the Green.

103

Canyon Country is
designed dendritically.
Each canyon leads into
another, and then
another. Their rivers
consume each other.
The Yampa River joins
another and becomes
the Green. The Green is
taken by the Colorado.
So is the San Juan, the
Dirty Devil, and the
Dolores.

The Green River, right,
twists below layers of
Navajo sandstone,
making it apparent why
this area is named
Labyrinth Canyon.
Childs refers to this
area when he writes,
"I could see erosion
and time and geometry
and my life all in the
same place."

the
Southwest's
Contrary
Land

Farther downstream, left, the Green River ambles past an area of Canyonlands National Park known as Fort Bottom.

TOM TILL

The Green is taken by the Colorado. So are the San Juan, the Dirty Devil, and the Dolores rivers.

If you follow it back to its source in the Wind River Range of Wyoming, the Green River is actually the largest and longest, outstretching even the Colorado. When I was 19 I guided my first river trip down the Green through Labyrinth and Stillwater canyons. Although completely unfamiliar with the terrain, I was flung into the job and was in charge. The food was less than perfect, because I was untrained. I didn't even bring coffee, because I did not like the taste of it, a fact that proved irritatingly irrelevant to the customers.

At one point, I took the clients on a hike up a dry canyon. I

had to admit that I had never been there, that I had never even been down the river — a confession that violated the code of all river guides. But I had to tell them, because I had never seen anything like this. I began tossing my hands around in the air, pointing and gesturing wildly. We got into the far amphitheaters of the canyon where our voices echoed sharply. Sandstone warped backwards against the sky, smooth as the lip of a ceramic pitcher. Hundreds of feet high, the walls were not straight or hard. They were round. Astounded, I could hardly speak. But I remember exactly what I did say.

"This is the place!" I told them.

They were half-drunk on it, too. But that wasn't enough. It

105

Mounds of swirled sandstone rise from the plateau in the Paria Canyon-Vermilion Cliffs Wilderness. "Its shapes of twisted stone and juniper are not what a person should expect of the earth," Childs declares.

107

"You can walk from Utah . . . to Paria Canyon to the Grand Canyon, and you will have passed through so much process and transformation that your notes will make it look as if you have walked the globe," Childs notes. The same neighborhood that produced the rocky swirls in the photograph on Page 106-107 lays claim to this scene, right, in Buckskin Gulch near its confluence in southern Utah with Paria Canyon.

was beyond being drunk or touching ecstasy. The place imbued
in me an absolute sense of being alive. I could see erosion and
time and geometry and my life all in the same place. Almost as if
I were commanding them to do something, I said, "This isn't a
vacation or some river trip. Do you see? This is *the place.*"

A few people looked at me, concerned. Others looked at me
with grinning sympathy. And one woman, I remember, did not
look at me at all. She stared at the canyon around us, shaking her
head slowly in disbelief. She saw it too.

□   □   □

There is a place called Grand Canyon. It is nothing like the
Green River, or the landscape of southern Utah. Grand Canyon
is hard. Abusive. Relentless. It is not my place. Maybe I was too
old when I first came to it. By my first multiple-week trip into the
Grand Canyon in my early 20s, I already belonged to the
twining, sensual shapes of Utah and elsewhere in northern
Arizona. Not to say that the Grand Canyon has not consumed
me at times. It has proven, like other canyons, to leave me mute
and mad with desire. But when I look over it from one of the
high rims, it seems too grand, too vast.

I have spent more than a hundred days down in the Grand
Canyon, sneaking through its shadows and deep cracks, yet I
have seen very little of what is really down there.

Even with all of its vastness, I find the Grand Canyon easier
to grasp than the sprawl of canyons elsewhere. It has clear
definitions: 600 yards wide at its narrowest section, 18 miles at
its widest, with an average depth of 5,000 feet or so; 277 miles
long, measured by the river in its pit; 287 species of birds, 1,500
species of plants; including its rims, about 1.2 million acres.

Most canyon systems not associated with the Grand
Canyon don't reveal these kinds of statistics. They are more
difficult to read, and fewer people are trying to figure them out.

The Grand Canyon fits statistics so well because it is a
solitary entity. It is a deep, singular plunge fed by 600 arterial
canyons, everything leading to the same destination, the
Colorado River. The Little Colorado River, in fact, is the only
stranger, entering the main gorge from the southeast,

RICHARD L. DANLEY

In the Grand Canyon,
left, Ribbon Falls sends
water onto a moss-
covered cone of
travertine, a form of
limestone, and supports
ferns and other water-
loving vegetation. The
falls lie in a side
canyon of Bright Angel
Canyon, which is one of
the Grand Canyon's
600 or so arteries.

109

JACK DYKINGA

Monument Creek has worked its way through granite in the Grand Canyon as it makes it way toward the Colorado River.

headwatered in New Mexico and eastern Arizona. The rest of the 599 canyons are strictly locals. They each tend to be remarkably deep and dark.

The place is filled with 90-degree angles. Its rocks, with the exception of the Bright Angel shale and a few other minor layers, are intensely solid. They stand like iron walls, hard against the world. The Grand Canyon is stern with its terraces and palisades. Nothing gentle in there.

Walking through it can be excruciating and frustrating, the careful calculations on routes seeming more like algebra than foot travel. I have spent time with two pioneer route finders in the Grand Canyon, Harvey Butchart and George Steck, and they both have worked as professional mathematicians. Steck, in particular, enjoys mingling his mathematics with the landscape, and he often speaks of equations in regard to natural features within the Canyon.

What distinguishes the geology of the Grand Canyon is that it is located in the basement of this land, but erosion has exposed it to daylight. The canyons to the east, and in Utah, are made of rocks thousands of feet above those of the Grand Canyon. In Utah, you can put your hand on sandstone, knowing that maybe 3,000 feet below, buried, is the hard, black schist that in the bottom of the Grand Canyon is exposed. The Grand Canyon is the underside of the canyon desert.

A canyon, by definition, is a place of resistance and accommodation at once. It is not a place at rest. Floods are carving it. Walls are caving in. Boulders are moving. The word "canyon" is as close to a verb as any landform can be. The Grand Canyon itself consists of aggressive resistance, with little accommodation. The rocks are hard enough that they beat back erosion. And erosion returns with ferocity. Nowhere else have I witnessed so many boulders and rocks spontaneously falling, exploding from ledge to ledge. If you want to catch erosion in the act, this is the place. Each piece of exposed land is fresh.

Once I was down toward the bottom of the Grand Canyon, alone. I had decided to spend my time in only one canyon, exploring its arms and rims and floors. Late in my stay, only a few

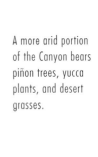

A more arid portion
of the Canyon bears
piñon trees, yucca
plants, and desert
grasses.

Acting mellow, Tapeats Creek shows side decorations of crimson monkeyflowers, watercress (with the white flowers), and granite. Elsewhere, the creek has cut a deep gorge, one of the Grand Canyon's arteries.

113

Geology earned an 'A' when it formed the shapes and colors in this area of the Colorado Plateau called the Waterpocket Fold. The term waterpocket refers to basins formed as water erodes layers of sandstone. The term fold refers to an approximately 100-mile-long warp in the earth with one side (the west) about 7,000 feet higher than the sandstone layers on the other.

LAURENCE PARENT

were no angular chunks, no 90-degree angles. It was more like work done on a potter's wheel.

A breeze exited the corridor ahead of us, forced out by the narrowness. The breeze worked across our skin. Air conditioning. I asked for everyone to sit in the sand before entering this final, narrow stretch.

"Let's go through one at a time," I said. "Move slowly. Let your hands touch the walls. Whoever wants to, go first." We sat for a few minutes in the quiet, until one person rose and walked. We watched him as his body disappeared, reappeared, and disappeared again around the tight bends. Then another person.

Finally, one student was left with me. After the last person was out of sight, she told me about her dreams, how she had seen this place before. At the age of six she first dreamed of this cave-like passage, and of the air nearly damp. She looked at me and said, "Go ahead. I'd like to be the last one through." So I did. I walked into the cool air. In times past, I had to wade through old floodwater to get through this canyon. Now, there was only a bit of moisture to the sand. Smooth bulges of rock closed me in.

After a hundred feet, the canyon suddenly opened. It certainly could have closed there, finishing itself off in a dark crevice. But instead, it revealed a huge, open chamber full of sunlight and the soft leaves of boxelder trees. At least 300 feet deep, several hundred yards wide, it was a secret hole full of life, no way in but through the dark corridor.

Half an hour passed until the woman behind me finally arrived. She wandered into the massive chamber, her eyes wide.

We all sat for over an hour. We explored for the same amount of time. This was the Shangri-La of the desert canyons, the unknown place. Maybe from an airplane you could find it, flying low directly over the top. Otherwise, you have to walk up and down every canyon, not being turned back by false dead ends. This dramatic, open room was so different from the Grand Canyon, so different from Lake Powell, so different from the Green River, so different from the winter desert elsewhere in Utah.

Later, as I read the notes and journals of my students, I came across an entry by a young man named Nathan Waggoner. A

117

Stone dominates scenes in the Grand Staircase/ Escalante National Monument. Wingate sandstone forms a sheer cliff in Long Valley.

the
Southwest's
Contrary
Land

118

number of his lines I read over and over again. They were:

> The Hebrew clansmen tied
> a rope to the high priest's foot when
> he entered the temple of Jerusalem.
>
> So in case he died they
> could drag him out without
> entering their most sacred place.
>
> The million to one chance that
> his heart might stop
> while uttering the name of God.
>
> So much power in the proclamation
> of a single word.
> All wrapped in the hidden knowledge of vowels.
>
> Here there are no words
> Just the gentle track of a star.
>
> Where is the rope around my ankle?
> Who is standing on the other side
> waiting to rid this place of my overwhelmed body?
>
> I am alone
> And the ceremony has
> long since been silenced.

Why do I come here? Because of that very thing. Because in so many of its nooks and passageways I would expect a rope around my ankle to drag me out of a sacred place should I die there. Reading back over Nathan's writing, I remembered the woman on the first Green River trip I guided. I remembered her silence as she fully witnessed the canyon. It was the same kind of silence I read in my student's words. He saw it too.

■   ■   ■

TOM TILL

Elsewhere in the monument, a smoother, chocolate-striped Navajo sandstone forms the walls of Zebra Canyon, a slot below a dry, high desert plateau.

# A Mix of Boldness and Change

THE LOWER

COLORADO

RIVER CHAPTER 6

AND THE DESERT

MICHAEL COLLIER

The opening spread, Page 120, depicts author Craig Childs' words in this chapter: "The land around the lower Colorado River constantly exudes boldness. [It] . . . guarantees that the place will be full of change." Clockwise from top left are chollas and creosote bushes on a plain near the Bill Williams River; the confluence of the Bill Williams and Colorado rivers; the Algodones, also called Imperial, Dunes; and cattails in a marsh.

As the Colorado River nears the Sea of Cortés, right, its surroundings are a nearly barren tidal flat. Farther upstream, opposite page, a tributary of the Colorado, the Bill Williams River, forms the heart of the Havasu National Wildlife Refuge.

So dense was it that I held my hands forward. The sun was just rising, dissolving its light into heavy air. I had never seen fog so thick in the desert. It came from the Colorado River, only a few miles east of here, flowing up through dry, interlaced canyons. I felt my beard, and it was damp. Only 15 minutes earlier, I awoke to powdery frost. I sat up and found myself in a cold, dense cloud. Now, as I walked, I glimpsed rock hoodoos that appeared and vanished in the mist. Cliffs ascended and disappeared overhead.

I stopped, my hands out as if I were blindfolded. Nothing could be seen but the circle of ground around me. The fog closed, tightening against me. I listened for voices. For a bird. For the scuttle of a coyote. For wind.

There was nothing.

Was this the desert?

*Where am I?*

When the fog lifted, it did not actually rise. Instead, it flowed back to the river, re-threading the needles of canyons it had threaded before dawn. As the fog faded, the desert reappeared in its place.

The land around the lower Colorado River constantly exudes boldness. The presence of such distinct entities as river and desert guarantees that the place will be full of change. The following summer, I walked not far from where the fog had been. The

morning air was absolutely clear. In this clarity, stars the previous night had been so numerous and crisp that my eyes strained to take them in. I walked after sunrise, carrying a daypack.

In the first full light of the sun, the temperature accelerated beyond 100°F. I kept walking. Rods of stone lifted hundreds of feet around me, parts of a harsh, tormented landscape. In the flats between mountains, hot boulders sat alone as if dropped from the sky. Hardly a single plant grew across the broken, black surface. Every rock was sharp. I thought of what Hell might look like. And I thought of how few landscapes bring me so much bitter pleasure.

At noon I crawled into the shade of a paloverde tree and lay on my back. Too hot to nap. I looked to the side, studying small rocks and the fine, fallen paloverde leaves. I thought I heard something. A light whisper. I ignored it. When I turned my head to look straight up, I saw a great horned owl perched on a branch five feet above me.

At first I thought the bird must have been here when I crawled in. But that was not possible. It would have flown away.

Then I remembered hearing and ignoring the whisper of its landing. For an hour I lay there watching this owl, its head turning fluidly, its eyes molten. When I kept still enough, it closed its eyes. It finally flew away, and I remained.

A visitation, I thought. Visited by a desert god. I rose and walked back to the river.

□ □ □

A cold river flows into the desert. Where the two meet should be marked by bursts of steam and molten rock. The sinuous blue Colorado River and the low, anguished desert are so relentlessly alien to each other that violence should define their border. Instead, there is a vast silence. There are owls and fog. I think the place is made of witchcraft.

I don't know what else to call it. A haunting, enchanting landscape of impossibilities. I always feel as if something mystical is at work here. I don't mean crystals worn around the neck and palm reading. Not that kind of magic. There is something older here, something before our magic.

GEORGE H.H. HUEY

Another refuge extends for about 30 miles along the Colorado River. And yet, just beyond the marshy grasses and reeds, lie barren dunes. The refuge, north of Yuma, provides habitat for more than 250 bird species as well as for fox, bobcat, and mule deer.

the
Southwest's
Contrary
Land

124

The land quietly erupts as it nears the river. Sand dunes curl into spaces between canyons and great, sheer spires. I regularly have dreams about the desert around the lower Colorado River, the place between the Grand Canyon and the Sea of Cortés. I dream of crowded mountains abrupt as the sails of tall ships. I fly over them, arms outspread, dizzied by their cliffs, by their twisted volcanic cores and skyscraper pinnacles. My dreams are never geographically incorrect. The proportions are always identical to the real landscape here. All of my creativity and energy cannot conjure a land more preposterous than this, even in my sleep.

For five years I worked as a guide and field instructor along the lower Colorado River. After I quit the company, I was asked to come back and teach the training course for river instructors. In the few years I had been gone, I was told, people had lost enthusiasm for the river and the desert around it. Word had spread at the company that this was an unwanted job, that it was hot and desperate, that the river lay still as a rug. So I came back and taught. I had been told to emphasize safety and promptness and logistics. Instead, I told the trainees what I thought of this place. I took them for three days and toured them on foot into the canyons, and by canoes down the river. We went to places they would never take their students and clients. I wanted them to see what was out here, so that when they guided, their eyes would burn, and people would know that there is something to this place.

"You will never see anything like this again anywhere," I told them. "Not on this planet."

We went out one night with our canoes. The air sat still, hazy with moonlight. Distant peaks, dry as chalk, were barely visible. We drifted across a glass-smooth river through waves of cricket song.

Vegetation lined the water. When we saw a small break, we paddled our canoes into it. The break led to a passage, hardly the width of the boats. Reeds and cattails bent overhead, clogging the sky. We paddled for 15 minutes, 10 canoes following the backward curves of this channel, which delivered us into a still, backwater lake.

KERRICK JAMES

An adventurer paddles through Topock Gorge on the Colorado River.

Having been checked by numerous dams and slowed by flattening terrain, the Colorado River has lost the boldness of its mountain origins by this point, about 100 miles north of the Sea of Cortés.

127

The great egret, above right and opposite page, and the green heron are common residents of the marshes along the Colorado River.

As we entered, great blue herons launched into the air, flapping and screeching like brash, prehistoric creatures. They were hardly visible, their wings blanking out bits of stars. We floated among the dead standing branches of drowned mesquite trees. A gathering of white egrets lifted at once, ghosts rising to the dark.

Swamps, marshes, and flowing channels braid their way through the desert here. Cacophonous with waterfowl, the likes of the Bill Williams River, the Imperial Wildlife Refuge, and this place, called Adobe Lake, leave streamers of deep vegetation in the driest, hottest pieces of North America. It is solid irony.

We sat in our canoes, allowing the birds to settle. No one spoke. Each person remained absolutely still, so that not even wrinkling clothing could be heard. That night, as we set our camp, I told them that never once did I believe that this was a common landscape. This is a place of sorcery.

□   □   □

The last time I came out to the river, I planned specifically to cross from water to desert and back, examining the polarity. Regan and I paddled a canoe down Topock Gorge, through an area known as the Needles — California on the west shore, Arizona on the east.

Even from 100 feet toward the center of the river, we could smell the saturated scent of arrowweed among the cattails. We could hear the woody prattle of reeds in the wind. This was a strong April wind, coming from upstream.

To add to the general contrast, we had come on a weekend. Even though this is a national wildlife refuge, the river teemed with speedboats. Chrome glinted through plumes of spraying water. Sometimes 10 or 15 boats passed every minute, full throttle. The passengers sat wind-whipped, clutching at their seats and their hats, immobilized. Bikinis on sinuous bodies and remarkably overweight men with incredible tans passed by the hundreds.

Besides the obvious recreational draw, there must be some lure from the visually unbelievable contrast of

BREAST FEATHER OF A GREAT BLUE HERON

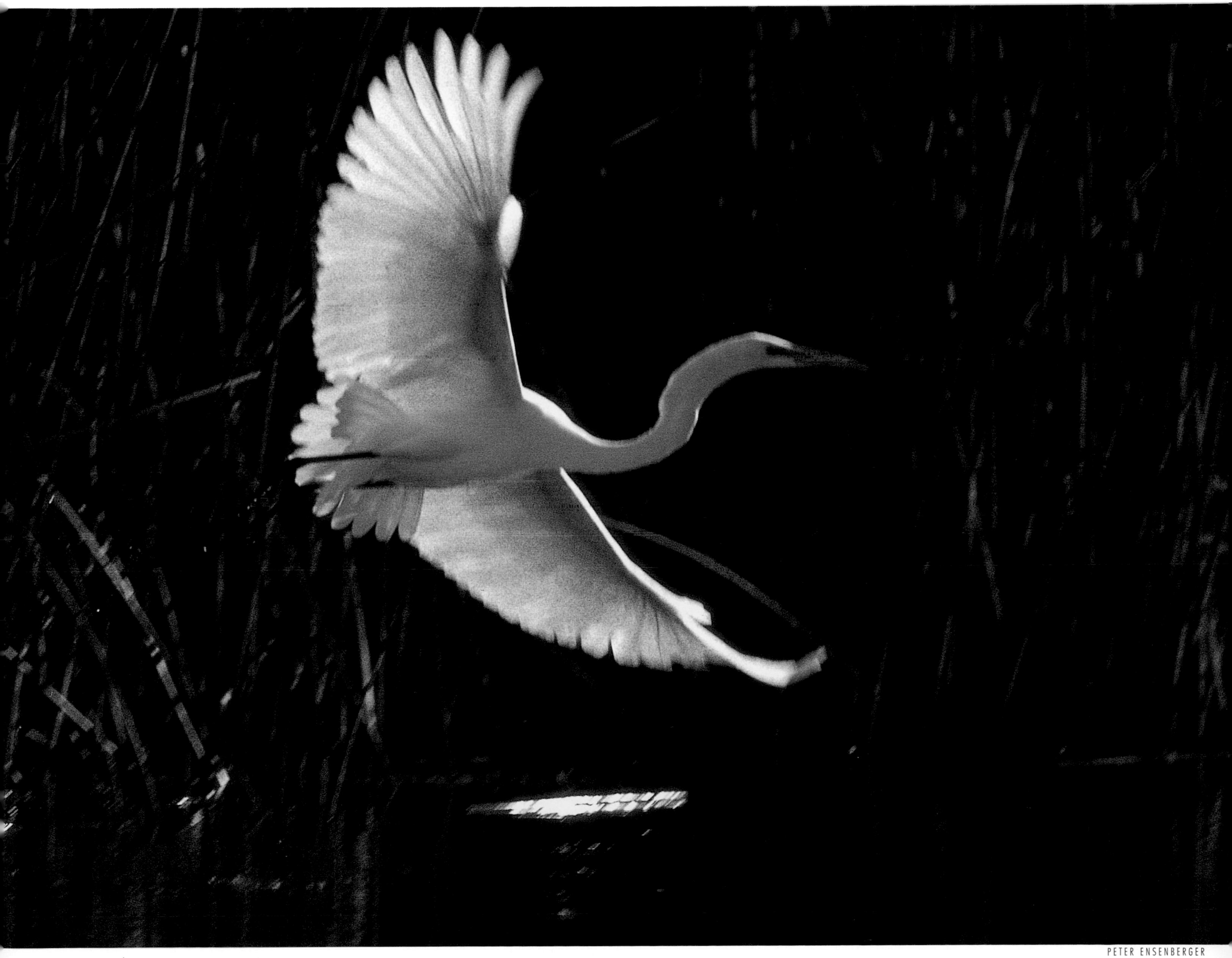

PETER ENSENBERGER

MICHAEL COLLIER

river and desert. I imagine that when they go home, besides the beer and the bikinis, they remember how bizarre it is to race across a river deep in such a dry land. The place gives the sense of traveling to the far edge of reality. At high speeds, engines unrestricted by mufflers, the edge seemed even farther.

Regan and I were part of this circus of gawking humanity, a canoe floating between the white streaks of speedboats. Regan, in the stern, led us down the center, then along the cliff shoreline. She drew the canoe right up to the rock face. We stowed paddles and reached out to hold onto it. Beneath us, clear water bulged upward, the current striking the bottom of the cliff and rising like a whale. Up with the current came swirling sand and tiny detritus. The cliff continued downward into the river, through changing shades of light, into darkness, and gone. Looking down, I felt the twinges of gulping vertigo.

◻   ◻   ◻

This strange alliance of water and desert has attracted much political and industrial attention. How could it not, as contradictory and alluring as it is? In 1985 the Central Arizona Project introduced a massive water transport system, carrying Colorado River water nearly 200 miles to Phoenix. During the construction, on days that reached 120 degrees, liquid nitrogen had to be brought in to cool and solidify the freshly-poured concrete.

Seventy percent of San Diego's water comes from this river. Almost the entire vegetable crop of California's Imperial Valley would return to sand without the contrivance of irrigation systems. Each Southwestern state relies upon the Colorado River, and when its waters were legislatively divided for ownership in 1922, a miscalculation in volume allowed states 30 percent more water than what actually flows. This miscalculation legally persists to today, resulting in anger, protest, and lawsuits.

Perhaps just the vision of this water created the original miscount. To

MICHAEL COLLIER

When distinct entities such as desert and river cohabit, the area will be full of contrast. Ocotillos, opposite page, lay claim to a dry, rocky knoll overlooking aquatic plants in the Colorado River. A swath of vegetation, left, follows the Bill Williams River as it trickles through the Rawhide Mountains.

CHOLLA CACTUS

come out here and find a river, you might think you could build a million cities right out of the rock. But you can't.

It seems random that the river is here. It could have come through the desert 10 miles to the east of here, or maybe 20 miles to the west. Or, if North America had a different tectonic history, there would be no river at all, the water escaping directly to the west, through Nevada and northern California. There isn't even much of a course this far south, the land hardly parting for the river to pass. To call this a gorge is technically inaccurate. The river simply flows, lost among mountains.

Being so close to sea level, it is easy to shift the river out of place. In 1888, an engineering mistake made while diverting water away from a railroad project sent the entire Colorado

131

River off to the east, across dry land. Immediately it ceased flowing to the sea, and began filling a below-sea-level basin 60 miles from its original course. That basin is the Salton Sea, slowly evaporating now that the river has been returned to its former path.

☐  ☐  ☐

Our canoe drifted through this random river channel. I suggested pulling over to hike, although if the shore was not a cliff, it was solid with vegetation.

"We can go through there," I said, pointing ahead.

"Can you define, 'go through there?'" Regan asked.

"Take our clothes off, jump in the river, swim through that mess of plants, pulling the canoe behind us, and find land," I explained.

"Thought so," she said. She maneuvered us into the vegetation, jamming the canoe — me first — into high reeds. Many stabbed into my ears and nostrils. Eventually we dragged the canoe through, holding branches of ironwood that hung over the water.

We climbed out, up chutes of hard volcanic rock, looking back down to deep, green inlets and coves hugging the land. About 400 feet directly above the river, we both crouched on a ledge. Bands of wind raked the water below. A flock of seagulls moved through, and we were high enough to look down on their backs. Stretched out for maybe a mile above the river, the flock looked like a stack of white typing paper launched into the wind.

Below the seagulls, white forks and rooster tails spread behind speedboats. Half a mile behind each speedboat, wakes washed the full width of the river. Seen from this far up, each wake pattern looked like the long, hooked tail feathers of a tropical bird. Then came the haphazard clanking of a Boy Scout flotilla. Aluminum canoes pointed all possible directions, colliding with each other, ricocheting away at odd angles. Jet skiers shot among the Boy Scouts the way wolves dart through a herd of deer.

Up here it was the wild hiss of wind across sharp rock. The wind yanked at my hair follicles, and I felt like my scalp was

RANDY PRENTICE

Canoeists enjoy the
solitude of the lower
Colorado River at
sunset.

133

Regulated by dams, the
Colorado River leaves
pockets of water as it
rises and falls.

being worked by a zealous barber. We had to shout to say anything. We climbed still higher to the bell tower of a pinnacle. The mountains around us were each pencil-pointed, their slopes made of flatirons pushing against one another. There was no sign of humanity back here. Looking away from the river, I saw layer upon layer of these mountains, a few of them half-swallowed by dunes.

Both of us sat to sketch in our journals. Regan, stooped in a slight shelter, looked like some bony plant growing in difficult rock. Her journal teetered on her knee. Long, dark hair unfurled and snapped. She reached out to pull it back.

There is no easy walking away from the river. Nothing flat or smooth. To cross this terrain is something like mountaineering, but making horizontal distance rather than vertical. In less than a mile, we became completely isolated from the river. Again, we huddled from the wind, our shoulders caved forward, heads bowed.

□　□　□

Seen from the air, there are three distinct zones to the lower Colorado, layered like a rainbow. The center is the river: blue. Next is the thin, but heavy band of plant life: green. Then the desert, which appears to last forever: black, rusty brown, and gray. The greenery is a dynamic corridor that defines the meeting of desert and river. With human alterations to the river by way of dams, diversions, and remodeled shoreline, this band has suffered greatly.

By some estimates, 80% of the best habitat left along the lower Colorado exists only within Mexico. The river in Mexico is often considered to be completely dead after passing through numerous dams in the United States. What is closer to the truth than complete death, is that the distant southern stretches of the Colorado River are verging on extraordinary life.

Technically, the Colorado River no longer flows to the Sea of Cortés in Mexico. Nine-tenths of the river water is taken by the U.S.,

going mostly to agriculture and households from Las Vegas to Phoenix to Los Angeles. The embarrassingly paltry remnants, heavy with pesticides and irrigation runoff, are drained through Mexico. What was once a majestic estuary at the delta has become a barren salt flat.

Dam releases during high-water years over the last few decades, and incidental projects by the U.S. Bureau of Reclamation, have fed bits of water back to this dry delta area. This water has spurred the growth of sudden forests. Endangered bird and fish species have returned, testament to the delta's tenacity and ability to rebound. At least one 60-mile length of river within these remote portions of Mexico is dense with native cottonwood and willow trees. Because this part of the river has not been channeled by bulldozers and riprap, as has much of the river just within the U.S., the water has been allowed to braid and fan out, feeding these forests. Unfortunately, the water reaching these burgeoning areas is little more than an accident. Changes in water use in the United States could halt what little reaches the delta, turning these new wetlands back into salt flats.

There is little environmental or political action toward protecting these budding wetlands and forests, compared, say, with the tremendous debate and money put into river restoration through the Grand Canyon. The Colorado River delta has by many been given up for long-dead. But it is still breathing, and these meager breaths have proven to be some of the richest environments left along the lower Colorado.

□　□　□

In the late afternoon we stashed our canoe along shore and carried backpacks into the desert, seeking a place to camp. We followed a broad, white-rocked wash decorated with bouquets of yellow brittlebush. Here, beyond the river, the sere environment differs harshly from the dense forests of willow, tamarisk, cottonwood, and arrowweed of the wetlands. It is more visual and tactile than ecological.

Once camp was set, Regan curled on a patch of coarse sand for a nap. I walked farther up the wash alone. No water. No daypack. Just a stroll. One of the most comforting places for me

These intricate patterns, opposite page, are crafted by Sea of Cortés tides, which flow into the Colorado River, pushing water up the slopes along the stream's channel. As the water retreats to the channel, it leaves its artwork on the flats.

DESERT LAVENDER

MICHAEL COLLIER

# A Desolate Desert
## of Rock and Water

IN THE HEAT OF AFTERNOON, FROM A RIDGE

ADRIEL HEISEY

2,000 feet above the desert floor, I watched a dust storm boiling out of Mexico. It heaved like a refinery explosion. Mile-high dust devils ascended from the ground.

I crouched behind a boulder to break a warm northern wind. It was from there that I saw a large bird of prey below — too far away to tell exactly what it was, hawk or eagle. It entered a rising pocket of hot air and swept upward at speeds that must have been dangerously ecstatic, even for a bird. It rose faster than could a propeller-driven airplane. In less than a minute it was 6,000 feet higher than where it had begun, turning arcs against the dead-blue sky. Without a single flap of wings, it sailed. It exited the thermal and glided down at a shallow angle. A mile away. Two miles away. Out of sight.

Without exerting more energy than one uses in an afternoon nap, without arguing through papers and currency at the border, this raptor crossed in a short time what would take me the next two weeks to traverse. I would walk the desert and hitch rides on roads to make the distance. This bird simply spread its wings and the desert laid open for it. I stared at the point where the bird had gone, even long after it disappeared.

This place, the lowest of the Sonoran Desert, speaks in clear tones. There are no questions. Just open land pierced by brief, studded mountains and the crossing of an animal now and then. I

come here often. To walk. To sit. To become lost in days or weeks of travel.

The sound of rock underfoot dominates this desert. A walk can hardly be accomplished without sounding like china being gruffly put away into cupboards. There comes the gravely, silverware crunch of walking in washes, and the plate-breaking ascents of steep, loose-rocked mountains. It was to the thumping of boulders shifting into each other that I began this journey. With a camp set along one of the high spines of the Ajo Mountains in southern Arizona, I walked the blocky ridges. Rocks constantly broke out from under my boots and tumbled away. Some ridges narrowed so much that I was left balancing across picket fences of volcanic rock. Below me, entire worlds of canyons and peaks spread, gathering the wind, sending it up.

The Ajos, like many of the Sonoran Desert's mountains, are composed of only ridges. Like darting rabbits, sudden canyons shoot out from under them. The ridges are always sharp, always single-mindedly traveling high above the desert floor, ending abruptly at some plummet. Beyond each ridge and its council of canyons, the desert fans out smooth as calm ocean.

Coming from the north, I had hiked my gear to this top, setting camp at the mouth of a cave that looked west. Around me rose the bulk of the Ajo Mountains. With their great, smokestack pinnacles laid back at a common angle, they looked like a hundred Titanics sinking side by side.

In the late afternoon I came walking across one of the many intertwined ridges. In a small, natural shelter rested the skeleton of a young bighorn sheep. I crouched and looked in. This was exactly where the sheep had waited for death, out of sight of predators. Many of the bones had been half-covered with loose dirt, the work of burrowing rodents. Wood rats had come to gather the dry remains for their nests. The larger bones were left scattered across the ridge, wherever wood rats tired of carrying them. The smallest bones had been abandoned further away: knuckles, cervical vertebrae, toe bones.

Coyotes could never get up here. Too hidden for vultures, too rough for mountain lions, this was land for bighorn sheep. I

The opening spread, Page 140, depicts author Craig Childs' trek from a desert of rocky ledges and plains with crumbling boulders, top left and bottom right, to a desert of sea with beaches covered by millions of shells, top right, and smooth stones.

The mountain ranges come like swells or tides, rising across the desert plain. From his perch on the ridges of the Ajo Mountains, Childs could see Sierra del Rosario, opposite page off to the west in a drier land. The mountain's granite peaks cast long shadows over the dunes of the Gran Desierto (Grand Desert).

The top edge of a dune in the Gran Desierto, left, leads to Sierra del Rosario.

143

had watched three ewes earlier in the day. For an hour we stared at one another from their ridge to mine, puzzling each other out 100 yards apart.

This skeleton was on a razor edge 400 feet tall. I reached my hand into the shelter and lifted out the skull. It was light and solid, like a small, clay pot. The horns were only nubs. I thumbed through its vertebrae. A connected disk on each one marked this as a young animal, but definitely not a newborn. It was old enough for certain bones to begin naturally fusing toward maturity. Four or five months old maybe.

Perhaps its parent was killed when it was too young to wean, or it became separated from the group, or it broke a limb and was watched by its mother until death. I set the bones where I had found them and walked back toward camp, stepping over the slender ribs left by wood rats. This is how events are recorded here: bones and boulders.

□　□　□

For me, spending consecutive days and nights on ridge tops was like living along the girders of a skyscraper under construction. Other than the tracks and scat of bighorns, there was little sign of animal or plant life to obscure the exposed architecture. I followed long beams of rock, turning another direction at some riveted joint where peaks met. Even though it is eroding, the desert can be imagined to be building up from the floor with unfinished pieces extending toward the sky. Looking down from a perch, I saw the summit of a 1,000-foot protrusion of rock. Beside it stood an archipelago of followers: five smaller fins and peaks trailing across the desert, each rising as if in different stages of construction.

Every walk I took in this high, exposed land — if there is enough horizontal bulk to even call it land — was across teetering lines. A morning pee was delivered into a 500-foot drop. Evening thoughts were taken atop a steeple of volcanic rock, dinner eaten over a pitch black drop inches away. My body shifted to meet the requirements of the ridges. I found a different center of gravity, and a gait that altered easily, often placing my feet one directly in front of the other.

West of the Ajo range, water in the Cabeza Prieta is limited to rain-fed depressions. But saguaro cactus and paloverde trees do fine in such an environment.

At camp, I prepared an easy meal, soup with rice. The desert below was taken by long February shadows, the sun touching the horizon. Darkening crags led from my boots down a couple thousand feet to an expanse of flat, wash-scribbled land. Shadow and light broke and crossed and cloaked. The place looked like an artist's rendition of another planet. The sun set into the north flank of the Sierra del Pinacate in Mexico. Bolts of light came through every lesser mountain range between here and there. Behind me, to the east, night had come already, darkening the land.

On the third night camping atop this ridge, I found that no matter how many miles I covered during the day, I always returned to the same place to watch the sunset. After a day of spanning my body across precipices and scrambling fingernails into the rock, I found my silent ritual pleasing. Each night, before shaking out my sleeping bag and crawling in, I sat on this same point until moonlight emerged like a nocturnal animal lurking through the canyons below.

☐  ☐  ☐

So often, the desert is called awful names. I enjoy each one. Desolate. Barren. Godforsaken. Empty. These words ring like a stinging mantra in my head. There is no irony in them. Each describes the desert with honesty as a horrible place. But within the horror, in time spent, a person learns the languages and voices. The dialogue is unending. I have for so long dreamed of walking straight across this land, slowly for 300 miles, encountering each mountain range. I have dreamed of the clarity I would walk through.

When sunrise came, the eastern horizon vibrated with warmth. The sun rose on the nape of Baboquivari, a high, thumb-shaped mountain sacred to the Tohono O'odham. Being the highest object for hundreds of miles, it splintered the first direct light into the sky.

The mountain ranges like Baboquivari and Ajo come like swells or tides, rising across the desert plain. From east to west they become drier, their plant assemblage changing as if they were islands of different latitudes. Baboquivari has running water and rare fish. The Ajos, the next mountains west, have prominent

JACK DYKINGA

Yuccas and mesquite trees, opposite page, dot a grassy plain spread below Baboquivari Peak, which is catching the day's first light.

West of Baboquivari, left, the land assumes another look, accented by organ pipe cactus and teddybear cholla.

147

Depending on its size, a tinaja collects and holds water for days or weeks. Desert animals and human explorers plan their journeys in accordance with the locations of such depressions in the rock.

149

The saguaro cactus, right, begins developing arms when it is about 65 years old.

Organ pipe cactus, opposite page, has several tall, stately arms rising from a common base. The organ pipe, common in the desert of northwest Mexico, creeps into Arizona only in the plains near the Ajo range.

stymied by impossible drops or overwhelming plant life.

Down in one of these narrow canyons, the steep floor hardly lit even at noon, I found a juniper tree. It was huge, probably 400 or 500 years old. Its elephantine trunk barely fit the canyon, the rough, stone-battered wood woven in vines. At least 70 feet tall, the base 10 feet around, it was a monumental creature to find hiding in these depths. For those accustomed to the ancient trees of redwood and cedar, it might be hard to fathom, but this was an old growth forest. A forest of one. Dead limbs cluttered the floor, each one massive, almost too heavy to lift.

In this part of the world, scientists read the pollen gathered in ancient wood rat middens. Pollen tells the past. They found that 11,000 years ago, in much cooler, wetter times, forests of juniper, piñon, and Joshua trees covered what is now the upper Sonoran Desert. It was not until 9,000 years ago that the bulk of the woodlands was finally displaced, sent to higher country as the climate warmed. On the way up, leaving for cooler elevations, some of the trees became stuck in the dark cracks of desert mountains. Only in this kind of terrain could the Ice Age become trapped in the desert. Like the palms, the big nolinas, and the sycamores, this juniper tree found its own place. Seeds scattered so that here and there a juniper would grow within the Ajo Mountains.

Hours later I returned to my camp to prepare a meal. The camp was a ledge of small, sharp rocks — the remains of fallen, exploded boulders. From here I could look straight out from the Ajos. The next destination, the expansive desert, was what I saw, what I stared at as my food cooked. These worlds, the mountainside and the expansive desert, are so different in terrain and plant life, different in the way a person walks or sleeps or fixes a meal, different in the smell and texture, that new languages must be invented between one and the next. I slept that night with the language of vaulted canyons. Tomorrow I would descend and the words would change again.

☐  ☐  ☐

Walking the nearly-flat desert floor — when distant

DAVID W. LAZAROFF

Layer after layer of ridgelines stretch across the horizon. The plain richly vegetated with teddybear cholla, brittlebush and organ pipe cactus is a part of the Organ Pipe National Monument Just west of the Ajo Mountains.

155

Arizona. These are plants that the drier mountain ranges to the west cannot accommodate.

This cactus, along with the famous saguaro, and a number of other common, large plants here, first developed around 10 million years ago. Repeatedly the desert has come and gone, sending plants adapted for aridity into isolated dry areas as it recedes. Much as junipers, sycamores, and palms are driven away during the dry periods, the organ pipe had to retreat and wait during the cool times.

Having been born in the desert, my life constantly drawn toward dry, harsh places, I am reminded of the chance — the luck perhaps — of being alive during an interglacial period. Perhaps, born 10,000 years ago, I would have been equally as enchanted by glaciers and broad-leafed plants. But I think not. Like the organ pipe, I belong here. I would have been forced to some isolated place, huddled and sucking on stones for their dryness.

The Sonoran Desert has backed away for ice ages more times than we know, returning each time for maybe 10,000- or 20,000-year stays before the cold descends again. Now southern Arizona is 10,000 years into the heat after the last ice age. The organ pipes you see out here are enjoying a brief period of freedom as once again the earth dries and warms.

That night I slept among dense gatherings of organ pipe. They broke the stars for me, and kept the wind down. When sunrise came, I wrote in my journal that there is so much emotion related to the quality of light. It is as powerful and changing as music. Shadows of organ pipes stretched all over me. The shadows of dry, surrounding mountains stretched, too. Everything leaves stark lines here: the mark of the

FAN PALMS

Strawberry hedgehog cactus and white rock daisies, above left, form a bouquet amid rocks in the Organ Pipe National Monument. The monument's namesake cactus, above right, shares space with brittlebush.

Queen's wreath, opposite page, a desert vine that also grows in tropical forests, adds color to a stand of organ pipe cactus.

the Southwest's Contrary Land

156

landmark mountains are barely in view — is like navigating the open sea. Subtle vagaries alter the course bit by bit: a series of washes angled slightly away from the destination, a strong wind, the glare of the sun. Picking my landmarks, trying to stay on course, I left the mountains and walked southwest, peaks receding behind me.

The floor beneath the mountains became a cactus garden as the canyons unfolded onto the easy, endless slopes of desert. Stubby hedgehog cactus crowded among patches of dry grass and triangle-leaf bursage. Chollas of innumerable species occupied the bare ground above washes.

I walked differently in the presence of cholla cactus, with their spines able to sink deeply into flesh. I walked more flat-soled so that the spines would imbed underfoot rather than on the thinner side of the boot, and with heels straight, not swinging inward where they could deliver a caught cholla into my calf.

A cactus of less aggression, but greater physical stature, is the organ pipe cactus, its tall, stately arms rising 10 or 20 feet from a collective base. Most organ pipes exist only in Mexico, and this is one of the few places where they creep north into

JACK DYKINGA

Childs' journey takes
him from the Ajo range
to a desert basin
extending into Mexico's
Sierra Pinacate country.
Volcanic craters and
lava flows punctuate
the region.

159

across rotten embankments, each kept me from finding an easy rhythm.

I sat one evening in the quiet after the day winds ceased. There was no sound or motion from the desert. I traced my route in my head, thinking back across so many dry washes, and realized that I had found a cadence. The distance I had walked, turning in and out of cutbanks, proved the rhythm. I was sailing across the desert.

□   □   □

Friends of mine were driving into Mexico and I had arranged to meet them. I got a 40-mile boost courtesy of the internal combustion engine. After feeding me deviled eggs and beer out of an ice chest, they dropped me off along a dirt road not far south of the border, in a land of volcanic craters and lava fields. This was not far from the Ajo Mountains, which were still within view. The Ajos lead to an open desert basin where I had been walking. The basin extends to the southwest and rises again to Mexico's Sierra del Pinacate. The broad base of the Pinacate, a short distance into the state of Sonora, is rough with volcanoes. The youngest craters are only a few thousand years old. The lava flows are still distinct, hardly eroded. I started into this new territory alone, again.

The first crater I came to was Cerro Colorado, a pale, salmon-colored cone with intricately eroded slopes to the south. The flanks and shoulders carried stratified beds of volcanic ash. The ash had hardened to look like a soft sandstone, eroding into sweet, scalloped shapes similar to those of the canyon country of northern Arizona and southern Utah. But to the touch, it was not sandstone at all. Grains in sandstone are usually sorted into place by wind or water, which leaves a tight, coherent matrix. This ash had no such consistency. Placed by heat and pressure and coincidence, it crumbled easily whenever I reached for a hold.

I climbed through shell-shaped arroyos to the rim of the crater. The pit dropped hundreds of feet to a convex floor. To the north, directly across the crater, I could see the distant Ajo Mountains. Barely visible was a point called Montezuma's Head near where I had begun this trip. From there I could just make

desert. My body sharpens and hardens against these lines. In the times that I am away from here — the ice age of comfort coming to my life as I seek a house or a town — I feel my flesh turning soft, my sense of touch or smell dulling. I eat rich foods and sleep beneath gentle mounds of blankets. When I come here to walk, my senses ignite. It does not happen all at once, but stone by stone.

Soon I moved again. I noticed that if the washes weren't going exactly the direction I was, they became navigational distractions. One after the next they nudged me in their direction. A strong, conscious effort was needed to just walk across them and not follow their easy paths for a few harmless yards. Yards become miles during a day of foot travel. Miles become grave errors. So I angled away from the washes, clambering in and out of their brushy, dry banks hundreds of times over the course of a day. I fought with the urge to trail along the washes. The fighting, the forearm accidentally stuck into a catclaw bush (emerging with streaks of blood), the stumble

The Cerro Colorado crater, left and opposite page, in Mexico's Sierra Pinacate region, is a pale, salmon-colored cone. Erosion has etched graceful patterns into its southern slope, opposite page, and a setting sun magnifies its color. The cone is 2,460 feet in diameter and 360 feet high.

Many of the craters and lava flows in the Sierra Pinacate, right, are only a few thousands years old — enough time for teddy bear cactus and grasses to establish themselves. A decaying saguaro cactus, opposite page, lies on volcanic ash.

out the high ridgeline with the cave where I had slept, near the skeleton of a young bighorn gradually being disarticulated by wood rats.

West of Cerro Colorado, the ground turned from dust and sand into the manicured playing fields of black volcanic cinders. The sound of walking changed once more. It was now the crunch of dry beans beneath the boots. In places fingers of glossy-black lava flows sat frozen on the ground. Very few plants grew in this cinder soil. Only the larger ones took hold, so the place looked like a spartan, but carefully designed, arboretum. Ironwood trees, cholla, and paloverde dotted the terrain. Organ pipe cactus were replaced with the similar, but more angular senita cactus, their tops mopped with fuzzy spines.

To a lazy or an inexperienced eye, the desert rolls out and does not change. It is an eternity of drought. I have been here for so long, consumed with desire, my eye sharpened by the outlines of far mountains, that I cannot see anything but change. Each mountain and each wash carries its own name, even if they have never been named by humans. The transitions run steadily from east to west and north to south: wetter to drier, sharper to rounder, flatter to steeper. I use each mountain range as a marker to tell me of the adjusting plants and rocks. Even seemingly minor changes become the entire world turning over and over again. My personality easily alters as gray rock turns black over the miles, as organ pipes are replaced by senitas, as canyons feed into endless plains.

That night I spent time with the moon shadows of senita arms across black cinders. As I sat below, the arms wrapped up through the stars, holding the darkness as if these cactus were the bones of the night. Just less than a half moon gave a light that did not monopolize the sky, robbing the stars, but still showed the ground. Any desert looks surreal in moonlight, but these black, orderly grounds with islands of lone cactus and tortured profiles of lava became a dreamscape.

□　□　□

Sierra del Pinacate is an unusually smooth mountain for the Sonoran Desert. Around it are steep, crumbling mountains, but

JACK DYKINGA

Sand verbena also have their place on a rippled slope extending from Sierra del Rosario.

167

Some of the dunes rose 400 or 500 feet, their slender fins reshaping constantly in the wind. The wind came as a singular hiss, never stopping, only rising and falling in pitch. My body cast crisp shadows. I reached down to touch my own shadow, drawing my finger through the sand to see if the black would leak out like ink. Mine became the only strong shadow of anything for 20 miles, which seemed unreal and somehow perturbing. The dunes made a distressingly perfect beauty. I imagined that obsession and madness would result from too much of this. Or perhaps ecstasy, lunacy, enlightenment, whatever it is called.

My boots were clunky pieces of machinery. The leather squeaked in the dryness as I moved. I felt cumbersome and arrhythmic in this new landscape, but again, found my own rhythm. I sailed in and out of dunes and felt as if I never touched the ground.

I stopped over a deep basin of sand warping downward like a parabolic mirror — something huge, like a dish used by astronomers to read a distant nebula. Wind scribbled down its slopes carrying whirls of sand. When I looked up to its far edge I saw beyond it a transition I could not have been prepared for. At first, I did not know what it was. I had to squint and shade my eyes with a hand. I had to think about where I was and what this could possibly be. The words slipped from my mouth.

"The sea."

If it had a color, I am unable to describe it. It was a horizon of sunlight smartly reflecting every possible hue, cutting a surgical line across my retinas. Even 30 miles away, it immediately occupied each of my senses. In fact, my senses fused together at that moment. The Sea of Cortés. A desert of water. I walked forward.

□　□　□

When, days later, I finally arrived at the beach, I tried to categorize what lay ahead. I thought of Lake Powell resting against the cliffs of Navajo sandstone, but that image was too far away. Between the canyon country of the Four Corners and here lie too many transitions. The land recreates itself so many times

The desert of cactus and the desert of the sea meet at Ensenada Grande on the Sea of Cortés. The plants are cardon cactus. In the distance, Baja California can be seen on the sea's western edge.

169

Tidal pools at Puerto
Peñasco (Rocky Point),
Mexico, reflect the
day's final light.

171

Dawn spreads a hazy blue over the Sea of Cortés at an island named Espirito Santo.

173

Shells, right, seem to reach to infinity on a beach of the Sea of Cortés.
Except for its color, a mussel shell, opposite page, fits in with basaltic rocks off an island in the Sea of Cortés. Fused, multicolored rocks, following page, hold pools fed by a hot spring on the western edge of the sea.

the
Southwest's
Contrary
Land

174

that places are hardly comparable with the simple words of my language.

But the contrast is entirely unbroken. I realized then, walking toward the sea, that my thread of understanding has been my body. My body carried me across, from one end to the other, proof that these transitions are connected to each other.

Only at sunrise and sunset could I see Baja, little more than a wrinkle on the other side of the sea. During the day, as I first approached the water's edge, the sea extended without end, Baja invisible under direct sunlight. When I came down from the coarse sand and past clumps of dried seaweed, past the high-tide arrangement of bird feathers, I unlaced my boots and set them aside. My feet touched damp sand. The sound was that of walking across tissue paper.

I walked closer, listening to the rasp of gentle waves. The ground now had the texture of polished glass beads. Shells by the millions had washed up, rounded and smoothed. Bones had come up, too. I walked past the skull of a cormorant and the scattered, disconnected claws of crabs.

The weight of a continent pushed against my back. The weight of so much complexity, so much change. I walked past the spiral cores of shells. I walked past wafers of broken sand dollars. I walked down until a low, smooth wave caught my feet and my ankles. It felt like a strange animal, cold and alive.

When the wave turned around, sweeping back out, it pulled at me. In that one tug, the wave said everything that could not be known about physics and transformation and land and water. Mostly, though, it drew on my body, telling me about movement. It told me why I have come this far and why I will not stop. The wave rolled back to sea, grinning with vastness.

■  ■  ■

GEORGE H. H. HUEY

the
Southwest's
Contrary
Land

176